Praise for *Hard Pivot*

"In *Hard Pivot*, Apolo Ohno guides readers as they embark on their own journeys of transformation—offering valuable insight and techniques, and giving you the courage to keep moving forward."

BILLIE JEAN KING
WORLD-RENOWNED TENNIS CHAMPION & AUTHOR OF *ALL IN*

"Like so many of us who are professional and Olympic athletes, Apolo Ohno is no stranger to overcoming incredible obstacles, self-doubt, and failure—and all in the public eye. But it's his skill for applying these seemingly outward experiences to our inner worlds that is truly unique. *Hard Pivot* shows all of us how to discover what brings the most meaning and value to our lives and how to keep those things front and center as we face challenges or crossroads along the way."

JEREMY BLOOM
OLYMPIC SKIER, NFL PLAYER & AUTHOR OF *FUELED BY FAILURE*

"Apolo Ohno lives a life where he works every day to train his mind and spirit for peak performance. In this book he takes us there with him on that journey, and he shows us how we can do it too."

DAVID CRESWELL, PHD
PROFESSOR OF PSYCHOLOGY & NEUROSCIENCE, CARNEGIE MELLON UNIVERSITY

"As a culture, we tend to have a collective discomfort around endings and loss. And yet these painful experiences happen to each and every one of us at some point in our lives. Based upon Apolo Ohno's lived experience, *Hard Pivot* offers a courageous 'training program' that will help anyone navigate the inherent turbulence that arises when the game of life requires us to let go and face the reality that nothing is permanent."

DOUGLAS JOWDY, PHD
AUTHOR OF *THE GOLD MEDAL MIND*

"In these times of incredible uncertainty—for individuals and businesses alike—it's even more important for us to stand in our strength, adapt proactively, and lead with heart. With *Hard Pivot*, Apolo Ohno invites us to see the process as the prize itself and to show up again and again to what life has to teach and offer us."

LAUREN SALLATA
CHIEF MARKETING OFFICER FOR RICOH NORTH AMERICA &
FORMER CHIEF MARKETING OFFICER AT PANASONIC NORTH AMERICA

"We all experience struggle in our lives, especially around times of transition. With his Five Golden Principles, Apolo Ohno offers a system not only to find our way again but to rediscover our purpose."

DR. JASON WERSLAND
FOUNDER OF THERABODY

"All transitions come with challenge, and Apolo Ohno reminds us that it's within the struggle that we find growth. That we're in control of who we are and who we want to be. In *Hard Pivot*, he shows us, through his honesty and humility, that we are not defined by just one label, person, or profession—we can be many things. Apolo's refreshing take on the unknown, taking risks, and having the courage to do so will inspire and relate to readers from all walks of life, in any season of change."

JANET EVANS
FIVE-TIME OLYMPIC MEDALIST & MOTIVATIONAL SPEAKER

HARD PIVOT

Also by Apolo Ohno

Zero Regrets: Be Greater Than Yesterday

HARD PIVOT

Embrace Change.
Find Purpose.
Show Up Fully.

APOLO OHNO

sounds true
BOULDER, COLORADO

Sounds True
Boulder, CO 80306

Published 2022

Book design by Karen Polaski

The wood used to produce this book is from
Forest Stewardship Council (FSC) certified forests,
recycled materials, or controlled wood.

Printed in the United States of America

BK06432

Original hardcover ISBN: 978-1-68364-932-8
Barnes & Noble signed edition ISBN: 978-1-64963-070-4
Books-A-Million signed edition ISBN: 978-1-64963-071-1

Library of Congress Cataloging-in-Publication Data

Names: Ohno, Apolo Anton, author.
Title: Hard pivot : embrace change, find purpose, show up fully / Apolo Ohno.
Description: Boulder, CO: Sounds True, 2022. | Includes bibliographical references.
Identifiers: LCCN 2021043176 (print) | LCCN 2021043177 (ebook) | ISBN
    9781683649328 (hardcover) | ISBN 9781683649335 (ebook)
Subjects: LCSH: Change (Psychology) | Motivation (Psychology)
    | Perseverance (Ethics) | Self-realization.
Classification: LCC BF637.C4 O436 2022 (print) | LCC BF637.C4 (ebook) | DDC 158.1—dc23
LC record available at https://lccn.loc.gov/2021043176
LC ebook record available at https://lccn.loc.gov/2021043177

10 9 8 7 6 5 4 3 2 1

For my father,
my godmother Maria,
and my soulmate Bianca

Contents

INTRODUCTION

What Now?

The journey of a thousand miles starts
from beneath your feet.[1]

LAO TZU

I was just twenty-seven years old when I walked away from my dream, from the only life I had known for the previous fourteen years. Just twenty-seven when I shed the skin (or skin*suit*) that had come to define my entire identity: Apolo Ohno, Olympian. The fastest man on ice. *Sports Illustrated* cover model. Phenom. Champion.

I didn't make any sort of big announcement. There was no teary press conference, no parade in my hometown of Seattle, Washington. No major media interviews. In fact, I didn't really tell anybody what I was doing. But I knew I was done.

I had no doubt in my mind that I could still compete at a high level. If I'm being honest, I still feel that way. My confidence, which is one of the things that fueled my success as an athlete, hadn't wavered when I walked away from the sport. What changed was what was in my heart.

I knew how close to the sun I had flown all those years, and I remembered all the sacrifices I had made—all the outrageous things I'd demanded of myself in pursuit of my Olympic dream. And because I knew everything it took to achieve what I did on the ice and the toll those sacrifices exacted from me over four Olympic cycles—physically, mentally, and emotionally—I also knew what it would take for me to maintain and surpass that level of performance. And when I looked into the mirror, I knew it was time for a change.

I didn't know what it meant at the time, but I was headed for what I'd later call "the Great Divorce."

As an athlete, especially an Olympian, I knew that I'd been fortunate. I had the incredible honor of representing my country in three Olympic Games, and I had achieved my dream of becoming a champion. If they're lucky, most Olympians sacrifice and train like I did and only make one Olympic team, and most athletes who aspire to make the team give it everything they've got for years and years only to fall short of that goal.

Regardless of how much longevity and success one finds as a competitive athlete, the harsh truth is that all of us have a relatively short shelf life. The average NFL career is less than four years; the average professional baseball career is rarely more than six. And no matter what sport you're in, it hardly ever ends on your own terms. So many athletes reach the end of the line due to a limiting injury. Others get unceremoniously cut from the team, are traded to squads in locations they'd never choose to live, or stick around in diminishing roles as their abilities continue to decline. No matter how it happens, the end of an athlete's career rarely goes the way they'd planned. And when an athlete loses the one thing that's provided structure and purpose to their lives since they were a small child, they're forced to look into the mirror and ask questions that aren't easily answered. Questions like, *What now?*

Typically, we don't ask, *What now?* because we don't know how to *do* anything else. We ask because we don't know how to *be* anything else.

Losing a long-held identity can be frightening, even terrifying for some. I know it was for me. Although I was excited to embark on the next chapter in my journey, I was racked with self-doubt. I also felt lost and vulnerable in a way that I had never experienced before, and I responded by retreating into myself. Although I yearned for external guidance and approval—from a coach or my father—or at least to be understood by someone who could relate to what I was going through, I shut myself off from the outside world. I felt like an alien in a new land. I suffered many sleepless nights, trapped in the downward spiral of negative thoughts. In short, it felt like I was going to die.

In a way, part of me did. I had no idea how I was going to live with the gaping void that skating once filled in my life. *What now?* was merely the first in a series of seemingly impossible questions: *Who am I? Who do I want to be? What really matters in life?*

To discover the answers, I had to plunge into the unknown and make more mistakes than I care to remember, fail time and time again, and act in ways that I now consider embarrassing or foolish (more on all of that later in the book). I was twenty-seven—an age when many people have gained their first foothold in their professional and personal lives—but I felt like a kid, like I was starting life all over again.

HARD PIVOT

In speed skating, a *hard pivot* is an aggressive, high-speed turn executed at the corner of the rink. In a split second, a skater has to generate enough force, momentum, and pressure to carve a new path in the ice heading in the opposite direction—all while speeding up to forty miles per hour balancing on one leg and a sharpened blade barely a millimeter thick. I practiced this move countless times in training because messing it up in competition would spell disaster.

I didn't know it at the time, but the thousands of hours I spent practicing that turn—pivot after pivot, day after day—helped prepare me for my life's next act. Because pulling off that move required me to be utterly present and in the moment, every time. I wasn't thinking about the finish line. I wasn't keeping an eye on my opponents. It was just me and the blade and the ice.

Hard Pivot, this book, is a guide for anyone seeking to adapt and reinvent themselves in our rapidly changing, chaotic world. It's not a book only for athletes; it's for anyone who might find themselves at a crossroads in their life. Maybe you feel stuck in your job or chronically unfulfilled. Maybe your career path has been detoured by automation, corporate consolidation, or a deadly pandemic. Maybe you suffer from debilitating stress, anxiety, or conflicts in your personal relationships. Maybe you just want to mix things up and start fresh. Maybe you want to carve out a path for yourself that doesn't sacrifice your family life—time with your parents or children, for example. Whatever it is, *Hard Pivot* is meant to help you to identify what it is you want out of life and what it is that life wants out of you.

Hard Pivot is full of the tips and techniques I leaned on to make the most of my own period of self-analysis and transition, the same ones I use now in my work helping others navigate their own transformation. Along the way, I'll invite you to take a closer look at the concept of identity and explore the reasons why so many of us feel defined by our careers and relationships. After that, we'll take a closer look at goal setting, motivation, maintaining perspective, accountability, belief, and purpose, as well as how these things can help us reinvent ourselves and live with more happiness, good health, joy, and wonder. You'll also find lots of exercises and actionable takeaways designed to keep you on track, helping you steer clear of old habits while cultivating new ones. I'll also invite you to view challenges as opportunities for growth, learn to better address your fears, value your process over the end result, and develop your own definition and criteria for success. In short, it's going to be a lot of work, but it's also going to be a lot of fun.

THE FIVE GOLDEN PRINCIPLES

Reinvention is a process. There's no magic pill or shortcut and very few straight lines. That's why I came up with the following framework (covered in more detail in chapter 8)—to help keep me going in the right direction when the road starts to zigzag. I use these five principles daily because I've found that they work, even when I stumble. And because they work, I stumble less.

Gratitude Expressing gratitude as a daily practice enables us to maintain perspective, cultivate empathy, and alleviate stress.

Giving Selflessly giving our time, attention, and resources to others helps us transcend the limitations imposed by our egos.

Grit When we develop the mental stamina, resilience, and toughness to persevere through difficult challenges, we grow even stronger.

Gearing Up Preparing ourselves mentally and physically for the challenges ahead, we can level up our expectations and perform at our best.

Go We learn by doing, by taking the shot, by diving headfirst. By actually doing—by taking a *go* at it—we realize that failure isn't what we once thought it was, and we make a habit of picking ourselves up and trying again.

My hope is that these five principles (and the rest of this book) will help you get across the finish line and bring about the positive changes you yearn to make in life. It won't be easy, and there might be times along the way when you feel tempted to return to your old ways of living because pushing ahead toward the new you can be disorienting and disheartening. It's natural to doubt yourself from time to time, to convince yourself that the voices are right—that you aren't good enough, smart enough, wealthy enough, or whatever your particular "enough" is. And when that happens (as it will), I invite you to do something different: let your inner critic have its say, keep going, and remember that struggle is just part of the larger process.

As Douglas Malloch says in one of his poems, "Good timber does not grow with ease."[2] Sometimes our challenges and struggles are exactly what we need in order to grow and change, and there's always risk involved when we've decided to pivot. That's why speed skaters wear helmets. Of course, quite often our challenges are beyond our control (as much of life is), and when that happens, it's important to remember that we still have a say in how we respond. By harnessing our focus, our intentions, our will, and the incredible potential of the human mind, we can learn to make new choices, reinvent ourselves, and achieve way more than we ever thought possible.

Are you ready?

CHAPTER ONE

The Great Divorce

> When we are no longer able to change a situation,
> we are challenged to change ourselves.[1]
>
> VIKTOR FRANKL

Before you can reinvent yourself, you first have to decide who you want to be. I don't mean who other people want you to be or who you think you *should* be or who you think you deserve to be. You get to decide who you truly *want* to be, and you get to do so with your own criteria.

Most of us who grew up in the United States have been conditioned to define ourselves by our professions, even when our inclinations, desires, and skills aren't necessarily in line with our job title. Instinctually, we know that our work is only one part of who we are and that there are other less publicly recognized identities (as parents, volunteers, gardeners, or musicians) that are closer to our hearts. And even those labels don't tell the whole story.

PRACTICE
LISTING YOUR LABELS

This is a short exercise that we'll be revisiting a little later in the chapter. Simply jot down two lists on a piece of paper. On the first list, write down some things that people know you as: your job titles and roles in your community, for example (this list includes labels such as "FedEx driver," "unemployed accountant," "kids' soccer coach," and "guy with all the pink flamingos in his front yard"). For the second list, put down all the roles and labels that *you* identify yourself with ("father of two," "avid reader," "biker," "pinball enthusiast"). The two lists might overlap in some places, but you might be surprised at how different they are.

THE FIRST CHAPTER

Early on in my career as a speed skater, my father told me that life is a series of chapters, one leading to the next and that we lean on the lessons and insights we gain along the way to move forward into whatever comes next. That's hard to see when you're so immersed in one particular chapter of your life. I spent years and years believing that being an Olympian would be the primary identity that defined me, and it would take a long time for me to understand how limiting that perspective was. Of course, winning those medals opened doors for me that just aren't available to most people, and I'll be forever thankful for those earlier chapters of my life. And although some people will always know me first as an Olympian or a winner on *Dancing with the Stars* no matter what I do, I can now see those parts of my life with the first Golden Principle I listed a few pages back: gratitude. I might not identify as an Olympian anymore, but my father was right—those earlier chapters led to where I am today. And for that, I'm grateful. They were springboards that empowered me to pursue new paths, interests, and opportunities.

It took me a long time to gain this new perspective. I had pursued my competitive goals with such single-minded purpose that I didn't think too much about what the future held. On one hand, that single-mindedness is one of the reasons I was so successful as a speed skater; on the other, it's also why I was so ill-prepared for life when I retired from the sport. I was twenty-seven years old, but inside I felt seventeen. I had no academic education to speak of, no work experience, and no training in finance or business. I'd never developed other parts of my personality, gained any other skill sets, or pursued any source of purpose or meaning outside of speed skating. I had ignored or pushed everything else away from me (including intimate relationships) in pursuit of my ultimate goals.

The Olympics were my first great love. Even now, I can close my eyes and hear the hush that descends on the arena just before a race, so quiet I could almost hear my competitors' hearts beating as we took our marks. At that moment, I had no doubt whatsoever about my purpose or meaning in life. As a representative of my country, I was part of something bigger and more substantial than myself, and eight different times, I found myself standing on top of the world with millions of eyes on me, as an Olympic medal was placed around my neck. Those moments defined the entirety of my existence. I'm telling you all of this just to convey how profound the Great Divorce actually was for me.

I HAD CHOSEN TO DIVORCE MYSELF FROM MY PREVIOUS IDENTITY—THE ONE I FOOLISHLY THOUGHT WOULD CARRY ME THROUGH THE REST OF MY LIFE—BUT I HAD NO IDEA HOW TO GO ABOUT FORGING A NEW ONE.

My first aha moment was when I realized that my skills inside the ice rink weren't exactly transferable to other arenas in life. In business meetings, for example, I was eager and focused, but I was also lost at first, and my lack of experience in the industries I wanted to be involved with made me feel insecure and small. And then I noticed that the further I got away from skating, the less frequently I was asked to do speaking engagements (and be paid for doing them). On top of it all, I struggled with the basics of how to arrange my day. For the longest time, my days had been structured around the team's training program, and I was no longer in the same world with those teammates and coaches—people I'd leaned on for years and years.

In short, the reality of the Great Divorce hit me harder each successive day. Everything I had accomplished—everything I *was*—seemed relegated to the past, mere scratches on a result sheet that would be eventually forgotten in time. It's hard to describe the confusion, uncertainty, and fear I experienced as a result of that realization.

I didn't know what else I was good at doing or if I was good enough to succeed at anything else. I had chosen to divorce myself from my previous identity—the one I foolishly thought would carry me through the rest of my life—but I had no idea how to go about forging a new one. I didn't know if anything could ever replace the passion I once had, the drive to succeed, or the incredibly powerful sense of identity I had with my sport. But I did know that whatever I was going to do next would be done away from the ice.

When I retired from skating, the thing I craved most and hungered to show the world was that there was so much more to me than what I did on the ice. I desperately wanted people to recognize me for the skills and strengths that I had outside of the Olympic sphere, even though I wasn't quite sure what those were just yet. I didn't want to go out to eat and just be recognized as Apolo Ohno, "Former Olympian Speed Skater." I didn't want people to look at me as just another dumb jock. I didn't want to be just the latest face on a Wheaties box, one that would be replaced in short order and eventually vanished from public consciousness.

What I'm pointing out is that my pursuit for a new identity didn't have the healthiest start. It was reactionary, ego-driven, and fueled by my *FOPO* (fears of other people's opinions). Going back to the opening of this chapter, I wasn't looking into who I truly wanted to be; I was focused on what other people thought of me and what I mistakenly believed they expected from me. I was still terrified of letting others down—my father, my friends, my teammates, and my fans. Basically, I forgot about me. I forgot about the one person I should have been prioritizing the whole time.

A NEW PIVOT

Right after the Great Divorce, the first thing I did was sprint as far away from the United States as I could, mostly to Asia. I'd always been enamored of other cultures—the food, people, sights, and sounds. I loved being near the Buddhist monks in Thailand, gazing out upon rice fields in China, and enjoying the peace and tranquility of *onsen* baths throughout Japan, where my ancestors on my father's side are from.

While I was in Asia still working out what I wanted to do next in life, I haphazardly began pursuing various business interests, none of which I knew anything about. I started with rare earth minerals, and then I moved into cross-border investments, manufacturing, real estate, infrastructure, mining, shipping, and tech (among other industries). Although my experience in these arenas was quite limited, my curiosity and willingness to learn was quite high. Furthermore, I'd long since practiced the art of surrounding myself with experts, and immersing myself in their expertise jump-started my education and helped me cultivate important relationships along the way. Once I got started, I said yes to basically everything that came my way. That time in my life was quite disorienting and sometimes frightening, but it was also exhilarating. I was starting from scratch, something I hadn't done since I was a kid.

As I'd shown with skating all those years ago, I proved to be a quick study. And because I'd trained as a sprinter for so long, I was accustomed to going really fast to figure out what I had to accomplish and how. I worked at warp speed to learn everything I could about these businesses so I wouldn't walk into a meeting with, say, a bunch of investment bankers and encounter puzzled looks on their faces when I opened my mouth—looks that would signal that I didn't belong in the room, that I was out of my depth, that I should go back to doing what I was most familiar with.

I wanted the respect of my business partners. I yearned for them to see me as a peer, as someone who knew what he was talking about, as someone whose perspective brought value to the conversation. To that end, I spent my waking hours studying these businesses, teaching myself everything I could about the various industries, and immersing myself in their worlds. It didn't take long for me to notice that the drive and relentlessness that enabled me to win Olympic medals was transferable to these new ventures. I was beginning to see that I was way more prepared for my reinvention than previously expected. Just because you pivot, it doesn't mean you should leave all your hard-earned skills behind. All your strengths and experiences are part of your transformation.

It dawned on me that I had become a great speed skater not simply because I was gifted as an athlete but because of my approach to the sport and certain attributes I used to my advantage. It was mostly my dedication to the mental and physical training that made me a great speed skater, not because I was somehow inherently special. It was because I did the work, because I refused to let anyone outwork me. My natural gifts had only gotten my skate in the door.

Realizing that I possessed attributes and inclinations within my control, and understanding that I could apply them to innumerable pursuits beyond the athletic realm, was a revelation for me. My thirst for knowledge, drive, mindset exercises, and visualization techniques was directly applicable to the world beyond skating, and it would enable me to gracefully pivot, shift my identity, and transform into the multifaceted person I truly was and wanted to be.

PRACTICE
WHAT'S IN A NAME?

Take a look at the two lists you made earlier in the chapter. For each label and role you put down (whether assigned to you by others or yourself), think about the qualities and attributes that you bring to each identity. Being a FedEx driver might not be the main way that you think of yourself, but this is your opportunity to ponder what you specifically bring to that job: the ability to focus on multiple details at once, for example. Or, say you're a kids' soccer coach or father of two; you might acknowledge all the compassion, humor, and cat-wrangling abilities you bring to those endeavors. Write these attributes down. In the process of reinventing yourself, it's important to recall and acknowledge all your natural gifts.

LIFE ISN'T A SPORT

Even though I came to my new ventures with certain qualities and attributes, I also realized that the world of business—and life in general—wasn't the same as the skating world. Sure, you can always gamify your life to some extent, but there are certain rules in sports that don't exist in the business arena, and vice versa. And many of the things that I'd leveraged to succeed in skating—my rage, insecurity, and terrible fear of failure, for example—weren't as useful in the realm of business.

I discovered that success in businesses is predicated on trust and authenticity and the relationships that trust and authenticity help foster. If you're not willing (or able) to show your authentic self, you'll have a lot more trouble succeeding in business. That's something I struggled with in the early days of my reinvention. I found it difficult to be transparent and show vulnerability because I was trained as a competitor to always wear a poker face and never show any sign of weakness. Unfortunately, closing yourself off in that way makes it a lot more challenging to empathize with others, and empathy is absolutely critical to success in business. Empathy is also something I've had to work at; it didn't come easy to me.

Neither did a lot of other things. Confidence, for example. And, even today, I still struggle with self-doubt, I'm way more insecure than I'm comfortable admitting, and I'm often inconsistent in how I practice and apply the principles I advocate for in this book. But here's the thing: even though I remain a work in progress, it's something I've come to accept about myself. And self-acceptance is key when it comes to empathizing with others.

Additionally, self-acceptance and self-love are critical in their own right. Most people, me included, have difficulty saying "I love you" to the person they see in the mirror every day, but learning to do so is incredibly empowering. For me, it goes beyond loving myself regardless of my mistakes and deficiencies; it's about loving who I *am* above and beyond everything I've *done*. I'm not just the Olympian, the medal winner, the entrepreneur, or anybody else's idea of who Apolo Ohno is supposed to be; I'm so much more than any of that. And so are you.

THE PATH FORWARD

The ice remains special to me, sacred even. When I walk into an arena and smell the Zamboni fumes and feel that familiar cool briskness across my face, I'm transported. There's something indescribably beautiful about the experience. So many memories are embedded in those senses.

Although I'm still connected to speed skating, growing into my new identity has also required me to keep the sport at arm's length. People are usually surprised when I tell them that I haven't skated properly since my last Olympics in 2010. I haven't laced those skates up even once, not even for a charity event or the sort of expected personal appearance in which you show up at a rink, wave to the crowd, take pictures with fans, and sign autographs. Sure, I've skated with rental skates from time to time, but not my *actual* skates.

When journalists ask me about my life today, I tend to answer them by focusing on attributes rather than my activities. So I'll say that I'm passionate. I'll say that I want to help people transform their lives. And if they ask me about my business endeavors, I'll say that I'm deeply committed to the environmental, social, and corporate governance (ESG) principles that guide ethical businesses today as well as to helping others embrace and embody those principles.

> WE'VE BEEN CONDITIONED TO THINK ABOUT OUR IDENTITY IN TERMS OF WHAT'S PRINTED ON OUR BUSINESS CARDS—WHAT WE DO INSTEAD OF WHO WE ACTUALLY ARE.

As I mentioned above, my path forward includes a lot of things that made me such a successful competitor, but I've also uncovered new attributes that are more applicable to who I want to be today. When it comes to skating or athletics in general, that means helping others who might benefit from practical advice (about physical training, nutrition, and so on) or from some guidance in the form of emotional or mental support (talking to them about self-imposed limitations or unhealthy expectations, for example). Beyond sports, I view my speaking engagements as opportunities to share my struggles and triumphs in order to connect to others and show them that we're not so different. If I can overcome my challenges, others can too.

At the time, skating for me was all about winning, setting records, and the acclaim that came with it all. But I see now that skating was just an earlier chapter that led to this one, and in this chapter I'm devoted to helping people believe in themselves, gain a healthier relationship with winning and losing, and learn new tools to transform themselves in order to achieve their true life goals. Part of how I do that is by sharing my story, especially the hardships and trials of the earlier part of my life, because I believe I'm an example that whatever has happened in your life before now—no matter your triumphs, struggles, or mistakes—you already possess some of the tools you'll need to navigate what's coming next.

FACING UNCERTAINTY

If you're reading this book, chances are you've experienced a Great Divorce of your own. If you haven't, perhaps you're seeking reinvention for a different reason. For many people, a new identity often means a new job or career, although it doesn't necessarily have to. As I mentioned at the beginning of this chapter, we've been conditioned to think about our identity in terms of what's printed on our business cards—what we *do* instead of who we actually *are*.

For many people, what they do to make a living isn't even a remote reflection of who they are inside or even what they like to do or enjoy in any capacity. Many see work simply as a means to an end, as the thing they have to endure for eight or more hours a day to provide for themselves and their families. They don't seek fulfillment through their work; they seek sustenance and survival. It's about paying the rent and the car note and putting food on the table. It's a way to get health insurance.

Working people have been dealing with this issue for a long time, but the COVID-19 pandemic threw an additional wrench into the works for millions of people when the unemployment rate in the United States reached levels not seen since the Great Depression almost one hundred years ago. Due to circumstances beyond their control, countless Americans were laid off, furloughed, or unable to find adequate work in their field. Seemingly overnight, these people were forced to put to bed whatever identity had been printed on their business card, name tag, or company badge because the title no longer applied.

How many of you (and your friends, family members, neighbors, and so on) were left scrambling, thinking, *That was the only thing I'm good at. That's what I've known. I haven't developed any other skill sets or strengths. Everything else feels foreign to me. What am I going to do?* And when there are mouths to feed and a mortgage to pay, a $1,200 relief check from the government doesn't go very far.

Even before the pandemic, it was clear that the days of learning a trade, securing a job, and staying with the same company until retirement are a distant memory. These days, it's common for folks to have two, three, or even four acts in their professional lives (or even more). Very few people remain at one job for more than four years. Some careers are getting phased out entirely, while others are being transformed by automation and other emergent technologies. Without a doubt, it's a stressful and frightening time.

If there's a silver lining to this instability and uncertainty, maybe it's that the answer to that profound *What now?* question I talked about in the introduction can basically be anything. Whatever you're facing, it's an opportunity to review, reflect, and renew. It's an opportunity to get curious to know yourself better—both the person you've been and the person you're about to become.

PRACTICE
STARTING SELF-INVENTORY

Grab a piece of paper and write down the following questions: "What am I good at? What am I passionate about? What was it that made me so good at the jobs I've had in the past" (or, if you're currently employed, the job you now have)? Maybe you're good at solving problems. Maybe, like me, you're passionate about helping people. Maybe you thrive when presented with new challenges or you get turned on when you're required to learn new skills. Leave lots of room to write your answers down and be as thorough and self-horn-blowing as you'll allow. Feel free to consult the list you worked on earlier in the chapter.

It's critically important to these exercises that you write your answers and thoughts down. Studies show that people who put their goals to paper are way more likely to achieve them than people who don't. As pro wrestling legend Diamond Dallas Page says, "Don't just think it, ink it."[2] That may sound corny, but it's fairly easy to remember (especially if you write it down).

These practices are meant to get you started on your path to reinvention. Before you transform your identity, you have to know yourself inside and out, and that takes a lot of reflection and self-acceptance as well. It can also involve some hard truths, so as you do the next practice, try to do so with as much clarity, openness, and self-love as you can muster. We'll talk more about the importance of that later in the book, but the key is to learn to see yourself clearly and honestly but without the unnecessary baggage of harsh self-judgment. To that end, try this exercise.

PRACTICE
ATTRIBUTES AND CHALLENGES

Take out your notebook or a scrap of paper and draw a line down the middle, making two columns. In the left-hand column, write down all the things you believe to be your most positive attributes. On the right side of the paper, list the things about yourself that you'd most like to change. For example, on the left you might mention things like "kindness," "intelligence," or "I always try really hard," and on the right things like "lack of confidence," "I get discouraged easily," or "education." Whatever's on your list is just for you to see, so feel free to write it out as comprehensively as you'd like. Flip to the next page to see an example from my own journal.

YOU'VE ALREADY BEGUN

Completing the initial practices in this chapter indicates that your journey of self-discovery and reinvention has already begun. In Joseph Campbell's words, you've been "called to the adventure."[3] The call to adventure is the first step along your journey—a journey in which each step is crucial toward the direction of your eventual transformation. That call means you're leaving the world you've known behind and entering the world to come—the realm of the unknown—where new challenges, trials, and opportunities await.

Along the way, don't be surprised when you stumble or come across unexpected detours. They're all part of the journey. There will also be times when you want to revert, go back to who you were before you

Positive Attributes	Things I'd like to Change
STRONG WORK ETHIC	NAGGING FEAR OF FAILURE
GRATEFUL	IMPATIENT
HUMANITARIAN	OBSESSIVE
MENTALLY TOUGH	DRIVEN BY EXTERNAL EXPECTATIONS
LOYAL	
CURIOUS	DISTRACTED
ANALYTICAL	FOPO (FEAR OF OTHER PEOPLE'S OPINIONS)
	INATTENTIVE

started this crazy adventure, and cling to whatever felt safe and predictable to your former identity. That's okay; that's all part of it too.

No matter what happens, all you need to do is treat yourself with as much understanding and kindness as possible and keep moving forward. Before long, you'll find that the further you travel away from your former comfort zone, the harder it becomes to go back there, and you'll start to build more and more confidence with each obstacle you weather. And your journey will likely be way more enjoyable (and transformative) if you accept that struggle, pain, and loss are all part of the adventure.

My journey to becoming an Olympian involved more ups and downs than most people would guess, and after I retired, I stumbled repeatedly on my path to reinvention. I blindly trusted the wrong people in some of my earliest real estate dealings, for example, which resulted in an incredible financial loss that I could have avoided had I done my due diligence. Still, it's hard to frame that mistake now as an abject failure because I learned a valuable lesson and became more resilient as a result. Without that experience, where would I be on my journey today? For that matter, without the hard-won lessons and remarkable resilience of our ancestors—thousands and thousands of generations of them—where would any of us be today?

I also want to acknowledge that it's totally natural to have doubts when you're on the path to reinvention. If you think about it, having doubt makes a lot of sense. Being in a new land means going without all the old landmarks you're accustomed to using, so it's normal to find yourself looking around from time to time, wondering where you are, and beating yourself up for getting so lost. When that happens, just keep putting one foot in front of the other and do your best to climb out of the swamp of negative self-talk. It's okay if you don't know where the road is headed sometimes (or even where your shoes are); if you focus on the journey itself and keep moving, you'll eventually arrive at your new identity. Like I said, you've already begun.

Whoever you are and wherever you've been, you set out on this journey with a set of attributes and gifts like nobody else's. Your purpose in life is unique, too, and that alone makes you magic. I don't know what that means for you specifically or where you'll end up as a result, but this book is meant to help you get there.

PIVOT POINTS

- You aren't just the sum of things you do, and you're way more than the labels people assign to you.
- When it comes to reinventing yourself, be sure to rely on the aspects of yourself under your control—your attributes, interests, and hard-won life lessons.
- Harness the tools you already possess to thrive through the challenges coming your way.
- Struggle and instability are opportunities for curiosity, reflection, and growth.
- Accepting who you are in the present moment will help you develop into the person you want to become.
- Detours and doubts are all part of the journey.

CHAPTER TWO

Your Starting Five

We live by each other and for each other.
Alone we can do so little. Together we can do so much.[1]

HELEN KELLER

Other than the relay competitions, speed skating is largely an individual sport. Though we train as a team and compete under the same flag, it's every person for themselves once the starting gun sounds. That being said, nobody reaches the Olympics by themselves.

Any athlete who competes in the world's ultimate athletic showcase didn't get there on talent alone, but on the shoulders of their family, friends, coaches, teammates, and advisors whose support and sacrifice enabled them to accomplish their dream. That support can take myriad forms—financial, emotional, educational, and so on—and it typically takes quite a bit of it for athletes to even make it to the Olympic trials. To paraphrase John Donne's famous line, nobody is an island, and that's true whether you apply the axiom to sports, politics, families, or life in general.

It certainly holds true in business. I learned fairly early on in my reinvention that you can't get very far on your own, and the relationships you forge make all the difference between success and failure. Unfortunately, this is one of the lessons I had to learn the hard way. I entered into a couple of business partnerships too hastily, and as a result I was exploited by people who didn't share my values or vision and who certainly didn't have my best interests in mind. But more on that later.

Jim Rohn was an entrepreneur and motivational speaker who was famous for his assertion that each of us is the average of the five people we spend the most time with.[2] In my experience, there's definitely a lot of truth in that. People who surround themselves with ambitious friends are more likely to pursue ambitions of their own, and artists of all kinds are more likely to dive into creative pursuits when they have other artists on their side. There's a flip side to that as well. Most of us are all too familiar with the consequences of spending too much time with lazy, unmotivated, or just all-around negative friends. For this reason, it's crucial to have people in your life who support you and embody the characteristics you want to manifest in your life.

If you're lucky, you got a good start in life with a nourishing, supportive family or at least one or two family members who lovingly aided you into adulthood. But even if you didn't, chances are that you can name a few friends, mentors, colleagues, or romantic partners along the way who've made all the difference in your life. And if you've ever been an athlete or competitor, you certainly know the value of supportive teammates and coaches. Like families, teams are excellent examples of wholes being greater than the sum of their parts.

TEAM BUILDING 101

There's nothing quite like working day in and day out, year after year, with the same group of people united with the purpose of achieving a noble and collective goal. I forged wonderful friendships with some of my Olympic teammates that last to this day, and I cherish the experiences I've shared with them on and off the ice. That being said, I've learned a lot about teams since retiring from the sport, and I sometimes wish I could go back and do better.

Without the support of my teammates, I never could have achieved what I did on the ice (not to mention the crucial assistance from my coaches, my sponsors, the US Olympic Training Center, my father, and so many others). Unfortunately, I didn't always get along with all of them, and there was a degree of resentment and jealousy on the team that I often felt guilty about. Rusty Smith, J. R. Celski, and Katherine Reutter all won multiple medals in short track at the same Games I competed in, but I was

YOUR STARTING FIVE   **23**

the one singled out by NBC and *Sports Illustrated*. I was the one they put on magazine covers and the front of Wheaties. I'm the one they called to compete on *Dancing with the Stars*. Of course, I took those opportunities and ran with them, but that doesn't mean it was fair to the others.

I learned a lot from that time in my life, and more from those teammates than they'll ever know, and many of those lessons have to do with being a good teammate and how to build and nourish a team that's based on mutual goals, trust, and support.

THE PEOPLE YOU WANT ON YOUR TEAM WILL NOT MERELY SUPPORT THE GROWTH THAT LEADS TO YOUR REINVENTION; THEY WILL CATALYZE IT.

The way people conceptualize what *team* means can vary widely, and there's certainly no one right way to go about team building. I have a friend who describes the process as *forming Voltron,* a reference to the cartoons and comics of the 1980s in which five intrepid space explorers unite to form one mega-badass intergalactic robot. These days, I think of my current team more as my *personal board of directors,* although I also like to use the *starting five* analogy from basketball because it alludes to the importance of having a variety of roles on the same team as well as the fact that the team does better when the ball is shared.

However you think about your team, pulling one together is as much an art as it is a science. It's not always about selecting the best individual players, but more the players who will work best *together.* Just as you wouldn't put five shot-blocking centers on the basketball court at the same time, you probably don't want to assemble a team in which everybody shares the exact same strengths. It's also crucial to keep in mind how the players relate to one another because chemistry is critical to a team's performance.

Ideally, your starting five or personal board of directors chooses you. That's just to say that who you'll want to make up your team will be obvious—they're trustworthy, they bring out the best in you, and they're willing to give you honest feedback when you're headed the wrong way.

They might very well be people you love and respect, but love and respect alone aren't always enough to foster the kind of transformative growth you're looking for. The people you want on your team will not merely support the growth that leads to your reinvention, they will catalyze it. They'll demand it of you. And they'll see your transformation as part of their own evolution because that's what it means to be on a team together.

PRACTICE
QUALITIES (PROS AND CONS)

Here's another two-column practice similar to the "Attributes and Challenges" exercise you did in chapter 1. For this practice, use the left-hand column to list the qualities you most appreciate in your closest confidantes (see example on page 26). These may be characteristics you want to emulate or simply aspects that complement your worldview or that vibe along a shared wavelength. These qualities can be fairly common (quirky sense of humor, loves animals, similar taste in music, for example), or they can be more abstract and hard to define (empathy, resilience, composure). It doesn't matter if your list is long or short. What matters is that you take the time to identify the things that attract you to others, especially the traits you hope to cultivate in yourself.

In the right-hand column, write down things that turn you off about people (see page 27). These should also be qualities that make for a poor match for what you wish to accomplish with your reinvention. Again, your examples can include anything relevant to you: lack of motivation, for example, or something more dire like cruelty or dishonesty.

Take a moment to review the two lists. Can you identify people in your life who embody the characteristics in each? They don't have to line up with all of them—that would be a tall order—but at least one or two of the qualities. Write down their names in the two columns. Do you see any surprises?

I like this exercise because it's a fairly straightforward way to identify the relationships you want to foster as well as those that might be counterproductive to your reinvention. If nothing else, you'll hopefully come away with a couple of names to begin assembling your own starting five.

MY PERSONAL BOARD OF DIRECTORS

I'm extraordinarily fortunate that my starting five hasn't changed much (if at all) since my Olympic days. My relationships with these guys have evolved over time, of course, but the core team remains the same. Maybe it's because I'm fiercely loyal or perhaps because I've been through the fire with each of them. I like to call them my personal board of directors, and I want to say a little about them here to give you a better idea of what a star starting five looks like.

My Dad (Yuki)

My father, Yuki, has been the single most important person in my life since the day I was born, so of course he makes my board of directors. I'm not exaggerating when I say that I owe everything to him, and the respect and gratitude I feel for my father for the innumerable sacrifices he made on my behalf is truly boundless.

LIKE A ZEN MASTER, OR A CROSS BETWEEN YODA AND MR. MIYAGI...

My dad came to America from Japan at the age of seventeen all by himself. He didn't speak the language, he had no money, no formal education, and no family to support him. He worked every job imaginable to make ends meet while studying accounting at night. At one point, my dad needed some extra money to cover his bills at the end of the month, so on a lark he decided to enter a hairdressing competition. As luck would have it, he won. And with the encouragement of some friends, my dad gave up accounting and went into the hair business full time. He started out small—one chair in someone else's salon—but in time he came to own and manage multiple salons of his own. And that's what he's doing to this day. He's been cutting hair and holding court in Seattle's Belltown neighborhood for more than forty years. He's like the mayor of Belltown.

My mother left the picture when I was just a baby and never returned, so my dad raised me all by himself. He and I are still very close, and no matter where I am, we speak at least three times a week.

Positive Qualities

Kind

Humble

Intelligent

Generous

Grounded

Appreciation of Nature

Love for Animals

Family Oriented

Positive Outlook

Strong Personal Values

<u>Challenging Qualities</u>

Arrogant
Unmotivated
Disrespectful
Culturally Insensitive
Pessimistic
Judgmental
Dishonest
Unimaginative
Rigid
Negligent

When I have a difficult decision to make or I'm feeling unsure about something in my life, he's the first person I reach out to for advice. Sometimes he'll text me sage advice or wise sayings seemingly out of nowhere. Here's an actual text he sent me: "Capability for life and understanding of life have been stolen by two thieves, which are regret of the past and fear of the future." That's how he's communicated with me since I was a child—like a Zen master, or a cross between Yoda from *Star Wars* and Mr. Miyagi from *The Karate Kid*.

My dad is definitely the reason why I have the cerebral nature I have as well as my work ethic. He's also why I value kindness, gratitude, and empathy so much. There have been times when I couldn't spend Christmas with him, so my dad would visit homeless shelters to eat and spend time with the people there because he knows how tough the holidays can be for those without family. He's always reminding me that everyone—no matter if you're a billionaire, homeless, a humble hair salon owner, or somewhere in between—is governed by the same core principles in life. "Don't forget," he tells me. "It doesn't matter where you are or what you have done or what you've lost in your life. These principles will always ring true. Whether you are here with us today or you're gone, the principles remain."

Ian Beck

I've known Ian since I was thirteen. He was my roommate on my very first international competition with the national team. Like me, Ian grew up in a single-parent household, and we bonded over that shared experience immediately. He also pushed me as a training partner for several years. Today, I'm proud to call Ian my best friend and business manager.

Ian is a very logical, analytical person. Like my dad, Ian is the voice of reason in my life, only Ian is way more direct. Those are excellent qualities to have in a manager. Whenever he sees me jump into a business venture, he's always the one pulling me back to reality. He doesn't get swept up in the excitement or emotion of things because, as my manager, it's Ian's job to be the levelheaded one and maintain the proper perspective so he can help me maximize my success. He's all about action and execution, and we balance each other perfectly—my yin to his yang.

The main reason I love working with Ian is because I have no doubt that he always has my best interests at heart, which isn't always true with agents and managers who are more intent on maximizing revenue. Ian evaluates each opportunity that comes my way to assess if it makes sense economically, but he's also making sure that it aligns with my values. We've been through a lot together, and with Ian by my side, I feel like there's nothing we can't accomplish.

John Schaeffer

John is the guy who taught me what the human body, mind, and spirit are capable of in the face of what seem like impossible challenges. I thought I was tough before I met John, but I wasn't. He's the one who showed me just how durable and powerful I can be, and he's also been somebody who's always held me accountable.

I had a lot to prove heading into the 2010 Olympic Games in Vancouver. People thought I'd lost my mojo in the field and that it was unlikely that I'd medal. I knew that I had to take an unconventional approach to my training in order to have much of a chance, which is how I found John, who had absolutely no background in skating. He was a powerlifter. Although he picked up some of the nuances of the sport, John came up with a new way of training that was focused on optimizing a handful of attributes—greater endurance, lactic capacity, lactic power, mental resilience, and so on.

John overhauled every aspect of my training, sleeping, and recovery. We changed the way we thought about the sport, down to how many times a day I'd train and how many pounds I'd compete at (twenty-three pounds lighter than my first Games in 2002). The training program John created for me had never been done before. If nothing else, I knew that none of my opponents were going to train as hard or with as much consistency and intensity as I was. With John's help, I remade my body and rewired my head, and as a result I did the unthinkable and won three medals at the 2010 Games: a silver and two bronze.

Doug Jowdy

I first met Doug Jowdy in 1999 when he was the head sports psychologist at the Olympic Training Center. I was seventeen years old and full of unpacked trauma and self-doubt, and I was barely getting by on my natural talent and instincts. I credit Doug for taking a brash kid with ADHD and turning him into a hyper-focused athlete who learned how to use his unresolved pain as fuel for competition. Without Doug's help, I doubt I would have ever become a champion.

For six months, I dove into all the visualization and mindfulness techniques Doug taught me—the same techniques I employ to succeed in my life today. Doug was the one who taught me how to focus on my breath, modify my heart rate, and enter flow states in which I wasn't as hindered by physical discomfort and pain while also performing at optimal awareness. Those are the techniques that helped me compete against physically mature men who were nearly twice my age, and I'm so thankful to Doug for teaching me and taking me to the next level.

David Creswell

David Creswell rounds out my starting five. Like Doug, David is a sports psychologist. He was part of the Olympic training team in '97 and '98, when I first arrived on the scene. David taught me a lot about the power of the mind, the value of self-reflection, and how disempowering negative self-talk and detrimental beliefs can be, especially when it comes to performance. David was also the person who first turned me on to journaling and using the practice to notice patterns in my life to enhance consistency. As you'll find in the next chapter, I'm still a big proponent of journaling.

In addition to teaching me about sports psychology, Buddhism, and Eastern philosophy, David showed me how they were applicable to my performance on the ice. I was fifteen years old when I met him (and perhaps not ready to receive all that wisdom), but if it weren't for what David taught me, I wouldn't have had any frame of reference for when I met Doug Jowdy a couple of years later and was ready to take my training more seriously. David also introduced me to Terry Orlick's *In Pursuit of Excellence*, W. Timothy Gallwey's *The Inner Game of Tennis*, Jon Kabat-Zinn's *Wherever You Go, There You Are*, and Robert M. Pirsig's *Zen and the Art of Motorcycle Maintenance*—all books that utterly changed my outlook on the sport and on life. David eventually went on to become a professor of psychology at Carnegie Mellon and, like the others, he continues to guide and advise me to this day.

So, that's my board of directors, my starting five: the man I most love and admire (my wise and devoted father), my best friend and trusted manager, the guy who transformed my training and physique to help me win three medals in 2010, and two sports psychologists who empowered me with the mind-body techniques that help me optimize success to this day.

I'm so fortunate to have all these wonderful people in my life. Although they're each quite different from one another, they all have a certain self-lessness in common—a selflessness that enabled my growth as a person and my success on the ice. I'm full of gratitude for every second I get to spend with them. I owe them everything, and I'd give everything I have to help them in any way.

YOUR STARTING FIVE AND THE IMPORTANCE OF DUE DILIGENCE

Hopefully, these last few pages have given you some helpful ideas about who to include on your own personal board of directors. You might already have a couple of people on the team, but maybe you need a few more to round out the five (although, just as a reminder, five is a sort of arbitrary number, and your own board could just as easily be larger or smaller).

PRACTICE
REVISIT THE LIST

Review the list of qualities (pros and cons) you wrote earlier in this chapter. After reading about my starting five and the qualities and irre-placeable value they've brought to my life, maybe you've thought of some changes you'd like to make to your two columns. Is there anybody else you'd like to add? Have you thought of any new positive or negative attributes that are worthy of consideration?

Part of why I'm inviting you to revisit those lists is because I want to stress the importance of doing your due diligence when assembling your board of directors. The same holds true, really, for anybody who plays a major role in your life, whether they be romantic partners or people you do business with. To that end, here's a cautionary tale about what can happen when you don't commit the time and effort it takes to vet such people.

I began angel investing and working in real estate right after my first Olympic Games in 2002. By 2006, I was putting energy and resources into these businesses a lot more aggressively, having no idea that the financial crisis was right around the corner. I was enticed to invest in a real estate group that was building luxury golf and vacation resorts, mostly because I misjudged their character and was blinded by the flashy lifestyle (fancy cars, suits, planes, you name it) they represented. And because of that, I was totally unaware that they'd over-leveraged themselves, all while I was continuing to invest in their company. The group eventually liquidated all their holdings and debt through bankruptcy, and I was out an unbelievable amount of money, and it wasn't money I could afford to lose.

In truth, I had zero financial cushion at the time. I had spent money on my family (including sending money to my grandmother in Japan), but I didn't have any reliable source of income at the time, and no sponsorships or endorsements. Almost overnight, I went from flying around the world in private airplanes to riding my bike to the ice rink to train so I could save money on gasoline. That's how nuts it was. In the end, I lost millions of dollars that I never got back, but the loss also crushed me psychologically. I knew that I should have investigated the group more before investing so much, but it was too late to do anything about it, and I felt as if the world had collapsed on my shoulders. It was so painful that I could hardly speak to anyone about it. Unfortunately, that experience is what it took for me to learn some basic lessons about business and the influential people you assemble in your life.

I COULDN'T HAVE REINVENTED MYSELF
AND GONE ON TO SUCCEED AS I HAVE
WITHOUT MY STARTING FIVE.

The bottom line is this: it's your responsibility to vet the people you get involved with. The world is full of wonderful folks, but it also has its share of swindlers, and it's often difficult to tell the difference. Look at Bernie Madoff. Look at Theranos. Elizabeth Holmes wooed the shrewdest investors in Silicon Valley into pumping $700 million into a technology that wasn't even real. My experience taught me that even when people seem successful and benevolent, in truth they could be downright shady. But it was my mistake to not check them out more thoroughly in the first place, and it's a mistake I'll never make again.

So that's another takeaway: all the loss, failure, and pain you've experienced is worth something. Even when it comes from your own mistakes, all that stuff is exactly what empowers you to persevere, adapt, and grow, just as the strongest of trees are the ones that had to fight for their share of food and air and light. Can you think of any inspiring success stories that don't involve great challenges or losses? I can't. The most stirring novels I've read involve characters who make poor choices, learn from their mistakes, and transform their worlds in ways that wouldn't have been possible on page one. People look at me and they see the Olympic medals, the commercials, the Wheaties box, and all of that. They don't see somebody who lost a fortune due to his own mistake, who felt like a complete failure for years, and who struggled to pick himself back up again.

But I couldn't have made it through any of that alone. I couldn't have reinvented myself and gone on to succeed as I have without my starting five, who've all experienced their own challenges and failures in life as well. In fact, their struggles are what enabled them to help me to the degree that they did.

PRACTICE
STRUGGLES AND TRIUMPHS

Let's take another look at your list of starting five candidates. Which of them have been through the fire in their life? How did they make it to the other side? What mistakes have they made that helped them reroute their life in a positive direction? What life lessons have they gleaned along the way that you can learn from?

PIVOT POINTS

- Be selective and mindful about who you surround yourself with. Their positives and negatives will rub off on you.
- Putting a team together isn't just a matter of assembling a bunch of star players. Chemistry is critical.
- Whatever you call your starting five, do your due diligence. Make sure the members of your team have your best interests in mind.
- It isn't about gathering a fan club. Pick people who will give you honest feedback and prioritize your growth.

CHAPTER THREE

Cultivating Belief

To be fully alive, fully human, and completely awake
is to be continually thrown out of the nest.[1]

PEMA CHÖDRÖN

I grew up with terrible self-doubt and an intense fear of failure. Considering what I've accomplished in life, people are often surprised to hear that, but it's true. The fact that I was able to do as well as I did, at least as an athlete, is a testament to human resilience and the expertise and kindness of my starting five. But it's also true that I could have accomplished way more had I not been held back by my own doubts and fears.

I think a lot of people can relate to this. It's not like any of us have cornered the market on self-criticism, negativity, or insecurity. Far too many of us feel like we're not enough, no matter what trials we've weathered, no matter how many external dragons we've left slain behind us in the dust. And while most of us are aware that we're too hard on ourselves, few of us are equipped with the tools to counter or move beyond the self-sabotaging thoughts and behaviors that hold us back, that keep us in our own personal bubbles of survival-thinking, and that prevent us from attaining our goals and actually thriving.

Learning to accept yourself—including those critical, naysaying, life-sucking parts of yourself—is an ongoing process. It doesn't happen overnight, nor does it have to. Like everything else in life, all you really have to do is be prepared to take the first step because once you do that, the journey has officially begun. And whatever personal transformation looks like to you, I'm fairly confident that you'll benefit from learning how to better deal with your own negativity, which is crucial when it comes to accepting and believing in yourself.

ESTABLISHING NEW HABITS

Research indicates it can take anywhere from 18 to 254 days (quite a range) to form a new habit.[2] What that says is that change is difficult even when change is your primary goal, although anybody who's ever made a New Year's resolution can tell you that. It's relatively easy to start out like gangbusters on that new diet or gym routine, but it's even easier to backslide into a previous comfortable routine.

Whether or not the practices below speak to you, it's crucial that you establish new habits of some sort to turn your reinvention from a mere idea to an active pursuit—something you're actually working toward, as opposed to just a list of more demands (that is, demands you haven't geared yourself up to meet). True gains are usually incremental and require consistent practice, and that's what helps us build genuine confidence and cultivate belief in ourselves. When we do that, it's a lot easier to keep moving forward, step-by-step, and perform at even higher levels. If you put in the work and do the reps, you'll gradually progress, and over time you'll build up more resistance to defeat and hardship—things that might have knocked you back to step 1 before.

PRACTICE
GETTING A GOOD START

One of my secrets (hint: it's not a secret) to establishing new habits and working toward what I want in life is a sort of master or "macro" habit, and it's getting a good start on the day. This is one of my primary ways of *gearing up* (one of the Five Golden Principles). I still suffer from self-defeating thoughts and behaviors, and I've found that if I wait to recognize that fact and delay my attempts to counter my own negativity until later in the day, I have to deal with a lot of extra momentum that makes the whole endeavor more of a project. In my experience, it's way easier to wake up a little earlier and take that part of the day to kick things off right, and this chapter includes some of the practices I use to do so.

I strongly believe that the best time to work with your mind is first thing in the morning, before the chaos and commotion of the day commences. When I'm on the West Coast, which is where I make my permanent home, I wake up anywhere between 5:00 and 6:00 a.m., when the world is still somewhat asleep (or at least before my fiancée and our dog get up), and sometimes even earlier than that. I use that first hour or so in the morning to clear my head, steer myself in a positive direction, and prime my mind for the tasks ahead. I recommend doing the same, simply because that's what works best for me, and I'm convinced that the morning is when most of us are our freshest, most vulnerable, and most open versions of ourselves. In that state, you can really influence the type of day you're going to have and set the stage, so to speak. So, if you're an early riser, great. If you're a late riser, that's fine too, as long as you can consistently carve out the time. Personally, I've found that the earlier I begin these practices, the better.

PRACTICE
MINIMIZING DISTRACTION

No matter when you get up, social media and the various temptations of connectivity and the internet make it too easy to start our days off in a distracted, unfocused fog. I get it. I'm also eager to check my text threads, find out what's happening on Instagram, or watch the newest dances on TikTok, but the truth is that once I enter that realm, it's hard for me to climb out and pay attention to what's actually more important to me (for example, goals). That's why my first habit is to keep my phone on airplane mode, place it on the other side of the room so I can't look at it first thing, or do whatever else it takes to avoid the temptation of hopping online immediately. Instead of that, I just get out of bed and try to get some natural light in my eyes, which is far better for me than the intense short-wavelength bluish light emitted from my cell phone.

Try it out for yourself and see what happens. Compare the alertness and clarity of your mind when you don't get on your devices soon after waking to those days when you hop on first thing in the morning.

Once you actually notice the difference, you'll be able to make a more informed decision about which state of mind you prefer.

PRACTICE
FEELING GRATITUDE

You might remember that gratitude is the first of my Five Golden Principles. No matter what challenges or misfortunes you face, gratitude will provide the fuel and perspective you need to carry on. As the great Sufi mystic Rumi wrote nearly eight hundred years ago, "Wear gratitude like a cloak, and it will feed every corner of your life."[3]

It's one thing to say "thank you" or *think* about what we're grateful for; it's another to actually *feel* gratitude. Take a moment to consider what gratitude actually feels like to you. What emotions or physical sensations come up when you're truly in touch with gratitude? Whatever that is for you, try to let those feelings infuse the next step of this practice, which is to simply acknowledge what you're grateful for and express that gratitude either aloud or on paper. My acknowledgments run the gamut from general ("I'm grateful that I woke up this morning") to more specific ("I'm grateful that I slept a full eight hours last night and feel refreshed and pain-free"), but they almost always have something to do with my health, relationships, or the experiences that got me to where I am today.

The length of your gratitude list isn't as important as how deeply you connect to the associated feelings and sensations. As with most of the practices in this book, shoot for quality over quantity.

PRACTICE
MEDITATING

After my short gratitude practice, I'll typically spend some time meditating, by which I just mean focusing on my breathing. Our breath has a lot of say in the quality of activity and states we enter, whether physical, emotional, spiritual, or mental. Especially when it comes to mental clarity, there are few physical practices you can do that match the power of regular meditation.

People have been meditating for thousands of years and describing its benefits for nearly as long, and there are countless ways to do it. For this exercise, even if you already have a meditation practice, I suggest keeping it simple: find a comfortable spot to sit with good posture and breathe in through your nose and out through your mouth. That's most of the practice, really. You can also notice how it feels to breathe in through your nostrils—the temperature of the air, for example, or the specific locations in your nose where you detect the movement of air. When you do this, it's natural for your mind to wander (that's just what minds do), but when you catch yourself thinking about one thing or the other, gently bring your attention back to the physical sensations of your breath entering and leaving your body. Some people also find it helpful to add a little gap between the in- and out-breaths: for example, in through the nose, hold for a couple of seconds; out through the mouth, hold for a couple of seconds. Try out different ways and see what works best for you.

If you're new to meditation, start off small—a couple of minutes, then five, then more if you can. There's nothing like kicking off the day with twenty or thirty minutes of meditation if you have the time.

PRACTICE
SETTING YOUR INTENTION

After meditating, I set my intention for how I'd like the day to go. This isn't the same thing as identifying the day's to-do list (which, personally, I probably did days before), but instead is more about getting clear about *how* I'd like to do those things. So my intention wouldn't be "catching up on emails and texts today" as much as it would be something like "being as present as I possibly can in all of my communications." That would mean not scrolling through my social media feeds or checking the stock ticker while I'm talking on the phone to a friend or business partner, for example. Instead, I'd pay close attention, ask questions, and try to express myself authentically and clearly.

It's best if you keep your intentions clear and actionable. "Feeling great today" isn't as memorable and doable as "fostering positive thinking when I get caught in negative self-talk." You might reuse the

DAILY GRATITUDE LIST

1. QUIET, CALM MOMENTS WITH MY TEA IN A.M.

2. MY DAD INSPIRES ME — VIA PHONE CALLS & TEXTS

3. SEEING OTHERS INSPIRED & READY FOR NEW CHALLENGES

TODAY'S ACCOMPLISHMENTS

1. MORNING RUN

2. CRUSH 3 MEETINGS

3. PODCASTS LINED UP TO TALK "HARD PIVOT"

INTENTION

1. BE PRESENT
2. GRATEFUL IN ALL INTERACTIONS
3. PURPOSE & VISION REMAIN CLEAR

SUCCESS LOOKS LIKE

1. AUTHENTIC & MEANINGFUL
       CONNECTION W/ OTHERS

2. BEING MINDFUL OF THE NATURAL
   BEAUTY AROUND

3. PATIENT

same intention for several days on end, or it might work better for you to kick off each day with a brand-new one or perhaps the one you used yesterday, but with a new twist.

PRACTICE
JOURNALING

Expressing gratitude and setting my intention fits right in with journaling. My journaling process is a modified version of Intelligent Change's *Five-Minute Journal*.[4] I simply list the three things I'm most grateful for, remind myself what I need to accomplish that day, clearly state my intention, and write down anything else that would help make the day a success. At the end of the day, I take another look at that morning's entry and reflect upon what went well, what was less than ideal, whether or not I accomplished my goals and why (or why not), and how I could have made the day better. For reference, I've included a typical entry from my own journal (on pages 40-41).

I suggest writing by hand when you use a journal. Handwriting is so embodied and tactile, and it requires more concentration than typing or texting. However you decide to use a journal, the most important thing is to articulate your goals, intentions, and so on. That way, you can refer to them later, track patterns and results, and greatly increase the likelihood of achieving your stated goals.

I'm not always on the ball with these practices—sometimes I do them for weeks or months on end, and then there are times when I'm more sporadic. My inconsistency often goes hand in hand with those times when I fall back into old habits of self-sabotage, but I always right myself at some point and get back at it. And although these practices all go great together, it's helpful to remember that even one or two of them are better than none at all. I might not be able to meditate for thirty minutes, for example, but I can usually carve out five or ten. And even if the only thing I can get to on a given morning is journaling, I've found that practice alone beneficial to my productivity. Although, the more I can do, the better. In combination, this set of short practices helps me slow down, clear my mind, connect with what's most important, and reduce the likelihood that I'll become preoccupied with things that don't essentially matter.

> WHEN WE CAN START OUR DAY WITH
> MORE CALM, CLARITY, AND CENTEREDNESS,
> WE'RE GENERALLY BETTER PREPARED
> TO HANDLE WHATEVER LIFE (OR OUR
> NUTTY BRAIN) THROWS AT US.

Slowing down is hard in today's world. Most of us are wired or trained to *go, go, go* from the moment we open our eyes in the morning until our head hits the pillow at night. If that sounds like you, then sitting down to meditate right after waking up is probably going to feel alien. But trust me: giving yourself the chance to reset and focus with these practices will truly help you face the day's challenges with poise, clarity, and presence.

In their terrific book, *Peak Performance*, Brad Stulberg and Steve Magness present their *growth equation*: stress + rest = growth.[5] Rest, they argue, is a critical component of the equation, because without taking the time to recover and reset, you'll eventually burn out. In addition, if you always go a hundred miles per hour every minute of every day without pausing to take a breath, you're never going to be able to recognize the micro-wins you've achieved or the incremental progress you've made along the way. Not to mention the fact that that kind of relentless intensity isn't going to make you a pleasant person to be around. So cut yourself a break. It's good for you.

Because one or more of these practices might not feel natural to you, it's important to do them first thing in the morning. You might not like meditating, and that's fine. Try it out for a week or two anyway. You don't have to be overly strict or rigid about how you go about these practices, and you certainly don't have to love them, but see what benefits come your way after committing to them for a set period of time. I can't guarantee it, but I'm pretty sure you'll find at least one new way to start your day with more focus, and you'll also get a lot better at holding yourself accountable for your priorities. That's crucial if you're truly committed to reinventing yourself.

HANDLING NEGATIVE THOUGHTS

Beginning your day with mindfulness, gratitude, and clear intentions will also help you combat any negative self-talk you might experience. Usually, our negative thoughts run unnoticed in the background, affecting our moods, perceptions, and behaviors just beneath the surface of our awareness. These practices will help bring attention to any negative self-talk you might suffer from, give you the opportunity to question and counter it, and also provide you a head start on dropping any self-sabotaging behaviors you're susceptible to. When we observe our thoughts and are more mindful of how we react to them, we can see what's actually happening in the world around us (as opposed to what we *think* is happening) and choose our actions more wisely. That's critical for making incremental progress.

Attempting to play Whack-a-Mole with our thoughts on the rare occasions that we notice them is simply exhausting; plus, the strategy doesn't work all that well in the first place. But when we can start our day with more calm, clarity, and centeredness, we're generally better prepared to handle whatever life (or our nutty brain) throws at us. Sometimes we're so busy beating our heads against the wall, trying to break through to the other side, that we fail to notice there was a door handy the entire time. These practices are your keys to that door.

I think a lot of us are fairly accustomed to criticizing ourselves for just about every perceived defect or mistake we make. Negative self-talk can easily seem like no big deal, but every time you say, *I'm not smart enough, I'm not good enough, I'm not beautiful enough, I always get it wrong,* or whatever your own personal messaging is, there's a part of you that's paying close attention to that offhanded or repeated comment, and that part of you feels and believes that the particular message is true. We don't want that. We don't want that part of you shying away from trying, from growing, or from reaching out for support. We want all parts on board with the reinvention, and reinventing yourself has very little to do with being unkind to who you are.

The practices I've offered in this chapter will not only help you notice the unhelpful or damaging things you tell yourself, they'll also empower you to replace negative thoughts with whatever messages you need to gradually become stronger, more confident, more resilient, and so on. The marginal gains you'll make by applying these new habits will give you even more confidence to keep chipping away at your goals. As Confucius said, "Whoever moves a mountain begins by carrying away small stones."[6] That's how it is with our beliefs, too. The longest journey still begins with a single step, so start small, and over time you'll be able to sprint or skate or fly into the reinvented you you're aiming for.

PERFECTION, PROGRESS, AND THE MEANING OF FAILURE

Sometimes the greatest obstacle we have to overcome is our own desire for perfection and our fear of falling short. More often than not, these two go together, and neither of them are particularly helpful when it comes to meeting our goals. In fact, when we expect too much of ourselves too early, it can increase the likelihood of failure—not because we're not gifted or prepared enough, but because we've set the standard unreasonably high. And when we place more emphasis on our anxieties than we do on our technique, love, and hard work, it diminishes our enjoyment and appreciation of the very endeavor we've committed them to.

Even though I know better, I'm regularly under the impression that I have to be perfect right out of the gate, no matter what I'm trying to do or how prepared I am for the challenge. Luckily, I know myself better now, and I've put practices in place to check my expectations. I also try to remember what truly successful people do, and that's to reframe the very notion of failure. For them, failure is just one aspect of a greater process. When you put failure into perspective, it's a lot easier to go out there and face your fears, take your licks, and recalibrate as you go along. That's how you learn and grow: by prioritizing progress over perfection.

QUITE OFTEN THE PEOPLE WHO FAIL THE MOST ARE SOME OF THE MOST SUCCESSFUL PEOPLE ON THE PLANET.

I'm not saying that you can't *want* to be perfect and that you can *never* be afraid of failure. That would just be setting you up for failure with another unreasonable expectation. What I'm recommending is this: put more of your focus on progress and forward momentum, keep moving in the direction you wish to go, and appreciate whatever marginal gain comes your way. Eventually, step-by-step, you'll see that you're actually getting somewhere, and that simple acknowledgment of your own progress will boost your confidence and will, in turn, help you commit even more to your journey.

Thomas Edison reportedly made thousands of unsuccessful attempts at inventing the light bulb. When asked how it felt to fail a thousand times, Edison replied, "I have gotten a lot of results! I found several thousand things that won't work."[7] Kareem Abdul-Jabbar missed close to half of the shots he put up in his career. Michael Jordan missed *more than half* of his shots. As mind-numbingly successful as the Harry Potter books and movies are, J. K. Rowling's first manuscript for the hit series was rejected a dozen times before finally landing with a publisher. That's all to say that people who fail are in good company, and quite often the people who fail the most are some of the most successful people on the planet. In the end, it's all part of the journey, and nobody remembers how many shots you missed, especially when you finally hit the one that matters.

When I competed, I almost always operated from a mindset of fear and inadequacy. The guys I was racing against—legendary skaters like Ahn Hyun-soo, Lee Ho-suk, and Lee Jung-su—were immensely talented and they had the medals to show for it. Even so, they weren't my most difficult opponent: I was. I never had much luck trying to boost myself with false confidence, but I did learn how to pull myself out of negative spirals and reframe the race. For example, telling myself, *I'm definitely going to win,* or *I'm going to smoke these guys,* usually backfired on me, but something like, *I've done the work, and that means I have the greatest possible chance at achieving what I set out to do,* yielded way better results. Over time, I learned to focus on what was under my control, to relax, and to give it my best shot.

I think that approach works best for anyone competing at the elite level, but you don't have to be an Olympic athlete to use it. Do the best you can and trust that your hard work will eventually pay off. And when you fail or fall short or make a mistake, find the lesson in it and use that information to improve. As you make gradual gains, you'll believe in yourself even more, and that will make you even more resilient to the difficult aspects of failure. It's as simple as that.

BELIEF AND FAITH

As a final note to this chapter, I'd be remiss if I didn't acknowledge that a lot of people cultivate belief through their religious or spiritual faith. I think that's great. Although I wasn't raised within any ongoing tradition or practice, my father took me to church from time to time, and my Japanese grandparents were Buddhist. Even though it never took with me, I certainly recognize the value and power of religion and spirituality.

If you're someone who draws strength from your faith, then by all means apply that to your reinvention. And if you believe in God—whatever God means to you—it would clearly be an oversight not to include God in your starting five. For millions of people, God is one star player who never misses.

PIVOT POINTS

- All of us struggle with negativity in some way. Self-acceptance takes work, and it doesn't happen overnight.
- Reinventing yourself requires establishing new habits.
- Always remember to slow down, rest, and give yourself a break.

- Failures and setbacks are a natural part of the greater process. Put most of your focus on how you're progressing (no matter how incremental) and establish forward momentum.
- Sometimes the people we know to be tremendously successful are also the people who've failed the most in life.
- Draw strength from your faith, whatever that means for you.

CHAPTER FOUR

The Work Is the Shortcut

No one was ever wise by chance.[1]

SENECA

In sports, winning and losing is often black and white. While the margin of victory can be determined by a lucky (or unlucky) bounce or an official's call, there's a finality to the result that is clear and incontrovertible. It's the ultimate results-driven business. In short track speed skating, a fraction of a second can mean the difference between winning a gold medal and finishing out of the medals entirely. A competitor can train an entire Olympic cycle for a race that takes about forty seconds to complete, finish mere inches behind the winner, and walk away from the race a loser. That's why it's important we don't take the *sports as life* analogy too far. It's also why we need to reframe the concepts of winning and losing entirely.

As four-time US Olympian Meb Keflezighi writes in *Meb for Mortals*, "When I race, I never lose. I either win or I learn. And winning doesn't always mean first place. Sometimes it means getting the best out of myself."[2] That's more of the attitude toward life we're looking for. Some might say that it's easy for Meb to live by those words, being the only man in history to win the Boston Marathon, the New York City Marathon, and an Olympic medal (silver) in the marathon. What else would he have to prove? I'd counter that it's Meb's very approach to competing that's made him so successful. Sometimes deemphasizing results is all it takes. You free yourself from expectations, you let it rip, and you end up performing your absolute best.

PRACTICE
LISTING WINS AND LOSSES

Here's another two-part practice that you'll follow up on later in the chapter. In your journal or on a stray piece of paper, make two columns: one for winning, one for losing. Jot down the most significant victories and losses of the past decade or so, things like job promotions due to good work, bombing interviews, romantic gains and struggles, debts paid off or accrued, or triumphs or challenges when it comes to physical fitness. Include an array of different types of wins and losses, and only include those things that involved you as an active participant (in other words, ruling out acts of God, environmental disasters, and other events or decisions beyond your control). Also try to limit your list of victories and losses to those that had a lasting impact on your life.

MISPLACED OBSESSION

I won my first national championship when I was just fourteen, and then I won it eleven more times, including nine in a row. I won ten gold medals at the World Championships, and then there are my various wins at the Olympics. Growing up, winning was everything to me. Not learning, not growing, not getting the best out of myself, but *winning*.

Foolishly, I thought that winning would silence the voice in my head that told me I would never live up to my father's (and others') expectations, that I wasn't training hard enough, and that I might never win anything else in my life again. That voice was full of fear. It kept me up late at night and woke me early in the morning. It's what got me to the rink before anybody else arrived and what kept me there long after everyone else had left. *You're not good enough,* the voice said. *You're never going to be good enough. There's always more to do. You've got to do more. You must try harder. You're not there yet. You're falling behind. You're getting too slow, too satisfied . . .*

Winning was supposed to shut that voice up, justify all the years I spent training like a maniac and make up for all the sacrifices I made in the pursuit of gold. Yet despite all the wins I accomplished, I only became more focused and haunted by my losses. They ate away at me and drove me to work even harder—harder than should have been possible, harder than was good for me—because the physical suffering that came from training that way was nothing in comparison to the anguish I felt when I lost. Winning was an obsession, an addiction. The more I won, the more I *had* to win.

The very first Olympic final I ever competed in was the 1,000 meters in Salt Lake City. I was only nineteen, but I was considered the favorite to win. I'd just appeared on the cover of *Sports Illustrated*'s Olympic preview issue, so all eyes were on me. On top of it all, 9/11 had happened just six months earlier. The United States was still in an extremely volatile and delicate mind space, and hardly anybody wanted to travel because they weren't sure if it was safe. People believed there were terrorist sleeper agents spread out across the country and were fearful of an attack at the Games (as had occurred six years earlier in Atlanta). All that's to say that there was a lot of fear, anger, and sadness to go around, which made me want to win even more. I felt a responsibility to lift my country's spirits by capturing the gold on home ice. In other words, I was under a lot of pressure.

I wanted to win that final so desperately. Not only because I had trained so hard for it and because the expectations were so high, but also because I wanted to show the world how resilient we were as Americans. The race wasn't just about me; it was about *us*. And so I went into that final confident that I could win it. I also believed in my heart that I *deserved* to win it.

But short track is an unpredictable sport, and crazy things happen all the time. In this case, I was in prime position to win the race as we all went into the final turn, but a collision occurred less than a hundred feet from the finish line. Along with three other skaters, I was thrown to the ice and into the boards, and I cut my leg badly in the process. Australian Steve Bradbury, who had been trailing the pack, avoided the carnage altogether and crossed the finish untouched for the gold. Somehow, in the midst of that chaos of bodies, I found the presence of mind to get back up and lunge across the line, skate first. And that's how I won my first Olympic medal, a silver.

"I DIDN'T LOSE THE GOLD.
I WON THE SILVER."

At first, I was furious and full of hate. I didn't say it out loud, but I felt convinced that the gold medal had been stolen from me. I didn't realize how badly I'd been cut until I got back to the locker room and saw my leg. I needed six stitches to close the gash, and they brought me out later to the medal ceremony in a wheelchair. Seeing that injury changed everything. Brent Hamula, a doctor and PT I'd been working with for four years, rushed in to attend to me, but the thing I remember most was the wild look on his face and him saying something like, "That was the most spectacular, crazy finish I've ever seen in my life!" I also remember the way that my father embraced me and how he told me how proud he was that I got up so quickly from such a devastating crash.

So when I had to face the media later on and one reporter asked me what it felt like to lose the gold like that, I was able to reply, "I didn't lose the gold. I won the silver." And the best part was, I meant it.

I realized that the expectation that I'd win gold (that I *had* to win gold) had all been created in my mind. I hadn't finished first, yet I walked away from that experience with something even better. I had something to be incredibly proud of—something I didn't *deserve*, but that I'd *earned*. I had given everything I had and was actually pleased with my effort. It was a new experience for me, and I felt full of gratitude and happiness. That loss/win was the greatest teaching tool I could imagine, and it was a major turning point in my approach to winning and losing.

2009 WORLD CHAMPIONSHIPS IN VIENNA

The championships in Vienna marked the first time in eleven years that another American–J. R. Celski–finished ahead of me in the overall rankings. I'd skated well, taking home gold in the 5,000-meter relay and silver in the 1,000 meters, but J. R. did better. He was only eighteen years old, and he looked like the future–genetically and technically, he was better at the sport than I was. Getting surpassed by J. R. at Vienna was both humbling and extremely motivating, and it's actually what sparked me to start the training with John Schaeffer that I talked about in chapter 2. It also inspired me to recapture the love for the sport I had when I first started competing. John and Ian helped me reshape my body and my approach to the sport. I dug deep, fully committed to the training, and, as a result, I won three medals at the Vancouver games that winter. Though I was nearing the end of my career, I learned that I still hadn't maxed out my potential, and I never would have known it had I not been beaten by J. R. Losing to him started the fire I needed to find out what I was truly made of.

PROCESS OVER PRIZE

So much has changed since I walked away from the rink. I have a much healthier relationship with winning and losing now, and I'm able to focus on the process over the prize, the journey over the point of arrival. When evaluating results these days, I just ask myself if I gave it my all. *Was I focused and purposeful? Did I conduct myself honorably?* If the answer to some of these questions is no, that's okay too, because that *no* helps me learn and grow, and it becomes the jumping off point for more questions: *What did I learn in the process? Why didn't I succeed? Is there a deeper meaning to extract from what happened? What could I have done better? Who did it right? What can I learn from them?*

In my opinion, too many of us are overly fixated on the prize, especially when it comes to external wealth and gain. At the same time, we suffer from internal poverty, with empty hearts and confused minds. Much of it comes from cultural conditioning. We're encouraged from all angles to stay on the hamster wheel for our entire lives because we believe that's what defines success. What's worse, most of us don't even know we're on the wheel. We've never even considered other options.

PRACTICE
REMEMBER YOUR DREAMS

Think of all the things you wanted to be as a kid: firefighter, astronaut, architect, artist, teacher, professional football player, magician, park ranger, veterinarian . . . Most of us grew up with one or more dreams of adult careers and lives that look nothing like what we ended up doing later on. For the most part, that's entirely natural. Chalk it up to changing notions of what's enjoyable and important in life as well as to the range of options presented to us by our communities and the larger societies we live in. But some of us remember our childhood dreams quite clearly, and their allure has never left us entirely. Maybe we were discouraged from certain paths because we were told they weren't lucrative enough, there weren't enough jobs available in those fields, or we weren't smart enough, fast enough, man (or woman) enough, or good enough in some other way. Reflect on this topic and write a few lines in your journal. If you would have had the ideal support as a child, what might have you done with your life? What would you have tried that you didn't, that perhaps you were steered away from? If you could go back and do it over again, what paths would you explore? Who with? And why? And if everything has gone according to plan for you and you're one of the lucky people who are blessed enough to remain happy with most of their major life events and decisions, write about that. What challenges did you overcome to attain your dream life? Who helped you along the way?

Once we stop buying into the limited promises of the rat race, what we call success varies widely from person to person. In fact, success means different things to people over the course of their lives.

One of my closest friends is a successful technology entrepreneur. He made a fortune, but it took a terrible toll on him. On the outside, he had everything a person was supposed to want and have in life, but on the inside, he told me, he felt empty. "I just thought it'd be different," he said. "I don't really want anything or need anything. What am I supposed to do with all of this money?" After some soul-searching, he successfully reinvented himself, finding true reward in putting his business acumen to helping others. It's no longer about dollar signs to him, but about shared values and helping people find their purpose. To me, he's a wonderful example of finding true success by questioning what winning and losing actually means to you and following your heart.

A DRAWER FULL OF MEDALS

Would you believe that I keep all my medals in a dresser drawer, even the Olympic ones? There's no display in my home, and it was only recently, after a friend asked if she could see them, that I took them out and really looked at them up close for the first time. I'm proud of what I accomplished in skating, and for the most part, I don't shy away from the attention those accomplishments bring me, but there's just something about those medals and what they represent. They're like shiny albatrosses, in a way. They're tokens of who I used to be and everything that was once so important to me. I don't want to rest on past laurels, on things that once emblematized what success meant to me. That's why I keep my medals in a drawer.

PRACTICE
DEFINING SUCCESS

What does success mean to you? How has what constitutes a win for you changed over time? Be sure to list any nontraditional successes–for example, any wins that went against the grain, that maybe didn't involve more money or other external signs of wealth. If it helps, block out a piece of paper with columns or circles of categories that pertain to your relevant goals: relationships, education, hobbies, health, fitness, and so on.

I don't want to say that there's something inherently wrong with large bank accounts, nice cars, new vacation houses, and so on, but I do believe that it's difficult to feel *free* when your primary focus is on the external trappings of wealth and victory. It's also a lot harder to acknowledge your self-doubts, share your vulnerabilities with others, truly face your fears, and own up to your mistakes so you can learn from them. When I was younger, I was more impressed with those external things, and I thought I was supposed to bottle everything else up inside, that I was supposed to hide anything about me that might come across as a weakness. I didn't want to tell a soul about my fears and insecurities. What if they thought I was weak or naive? What if they told me I'd never succeed away from the ice? So I lived for far longer than I should have with the armor of false bravado, and when you wear armor around like that for years, it will eventually wear you down.

We're given all sorts of reasons to hide ourselves, to mask our true nature and heartfelt desires—even from those closest to us—from an early age. I'm no different, and I've been just as prone to covering myself up as anyone. But at some point we need to realize that it's almost impossible to disguise ourselves and transform who we are at the same time.

You don't have to look back upon your life with regret. You're entering your second act, and there's plenty of time to course correct. This book is meant to help you do just that. Part of that correction involves taking a fresh approach to winning and losing, success and failure, and seeing (and believing) that failure is only that which impedes change, knowledge, and growth.

Mistakes, shortcomings, and losses are all part of the game. Lean into the process, embrace the journey, and do your best to accept whatever consequences come your way. Because if you only remain focused on results—results you likely don't have full control over—results will invariably control your emotional state, and only results will command your time, attention, and heart.

THERE IS NO SHORTCUT

I travel a lot, speaking to various groups and businesses. Last year, I was giving a presentation to a room full of founders and entrepreneurs, and one of them asked me how to stay consistently motivated over time. The question really got me thinking. While it might not seem like it on the surface, being an entrepreneur or a founder is similar to being an Olympic athlete. For one thing, you don't have a potential exit or acquisition until four or eight years into the life cycle of building a business, and you don't know if you ever will. Even so, you have to remain committed, motivated, passionate, and inspired, and your work ethic needs to remain consistent during that entire time if you want to have any chance of winning in the end.

In sports, business, and life, it's highly likely that the outcomes you experience don't match your prior expectations, even in success. In fact, I'd even go so far as to say that expectations aren't particularly helpful when it comes to achieving our goals. If you've ever spent time writing down or speaking aloud what you expect will happen to you four years from a given moment, most likely your expectation will either fall short, overshoot your target, or go off in some other direction entirely. If that's true, how can we maintain a sense of fulfillment and purpose and passion throughout the long process of trying to achieve our stated goals?

PRIORITIZING THE PROCESS MEANS COMMITTING TO THE PATH NO MATTER HOW MUCH IT DIVERGES FROM WHAT YOU EXPECTED.

I think it all comes back to self-examination, to asking yourself difficult questions—questions that don't always come with immediate answers. For example, *What are the actual needs driving this goal? Am I looking for more security? For more love? More freedom?* Understanding what drives you and paying attention to those needs throughout the ups and downs of life is crucial, especially when it comes to valuing process over prize. Living in a world of distraction in which every algorithm is designed to hijack your attention, the ability to focus on your process ultimately becomes a test of your self-discipline. It's not easy. But stick to what's most important and do the work. There isn't such a thing as a shortcut, but if there were, it would be the work. The work is the shortcut.

If you haven't realized it for yourself already, the path to your reinvention won't be a straight line. You might *want* to travel in a straight line, but good luck with that. The path curves with the terrain: you'll come across all the obligatory detours in life, you'll occasionally have to backtrack for one reason or another, and you'll get distracted. Prioritizing the process means committing to the path no matter how much it diverges from what you expected. The end goal is still important. I'm not saying that results don't matter, because they do, even when we prioritize the process. To quote former New York Jets head coach

Herman Edwards, "You play. To win. The game!"[3] If an archer didn't care about hitting the target, why wouldn't they just shoot arrows into the sky all day? Yet, it's possible to commit yourself to achieving stated goals while simultaneously maintaining perspective, and that perspective should keep in mind that winning doesn't define your self-worth and losing doesn't determine who you are. That might seem obvious to most people, but in practice it isn't.

It's easy to lose ourselves. It's easy to allow ego and our fear of other people's opinions to cloud our judgment and govern our decisions. It's easy to chase wins that mean little to us inside but seem to mean everything to the world. But winning feels awfully hollow when you're lost.

PRACTICE
REVIEWING YOUR WINS AND LOSSES

Revisit the first practice I suggested at the start of this chapter. Look at the significant wins and losses you wrote down in the two columns and reconsider them now. Are there any wins you'd like to add or remove? What losses would you change on the list? Finally, see if any of your major losses inspired actions or changes on your part that led to future wins. Make as many notes and alterations as you'd like and think about what those changes say about your current reinvention.

PIVOT POINTS

- Try to focus more on the process and less on results. Reframe what winning and losing mean to you.
- It's often the case that losing will help you way more than "winning" does.
- Celebrate your successes, and make sure you're the one who defines what success means to you.
- There is no shortcut. The work *is* the shortcut.
- Success and failure come and go, and they never define who you are.

CHAPTER FIVE

Relentless Curiosity

I have no special talent. I am only passionately curious.[1]

ALBERT EINSTEIN

If there's one thing that keeps us committed to the process while also helping us remain focused on the end goal, it's curiosity. Curiosity is incredibly important as we transform, reinvent, and pivot into new areas of our life—new areas that often feel daunting, uncertain, and scary because we don't know the outcomes yet. Curiosity helps us maintain a playful frame of exploration and makes sure we don't remain stuck in anxiety.

When we focus too much on playing to win the game, we can get caught up in dwelling on the consequences of losing. Humans tend to operate with a negativity bias. We mostly think about the potential for bad outcomes because that's how we survived as an evolving species, by always being alert to possible threats. Yet this mindset doesn't serve us in today's world because the majority of us no longer have to fight for daily survival.

Echoing the Meb Keflezighi quote from the last chapter, the singer Pitbull says, "There is no losing, only learning. There's no failure, only opportunities."[2] Both men are spot-on in reminding us that you can't really fail if you remain curious and open to the process, learn from your so-called loss, grow accordingly, and try again. If you can transform your attitude toward failure in this way, you'll see all your endeavors differently—not as events defined by one of only two clear-cut outcomes, but as open-ended adventures.

Of course, adventures have consequences. But instead of allowing fear to endlessly remind you of all the possible terrible consequences that could happen to you, you could trust that your curiosity will help you come up with creative solutions, no matter what. It's like that when we read an exciting novel or watch a thrilling movie or TV series—our curiosity keeps us glued to the unfolding events, biting our nails in anticipation of what's going to happen to the main character next. Will they be able to escape? Is this the end of the line for them? How will they ever be able to defeat the villain? We have no idea. But instead of closing the book or turning off the TV when things get dire, our curiosity keeps us invested in whatever is about to unfold.

What if we approached our life in the same way? Instead of habitually telling ourselves something like, *I just absolutely have to win this* _____ *because losing would be horrible,* what if we allowed our curiosity to step in and ask, *What's going to happen next?* That's how to make curiosity a superpower. The outcome is always unknown, and that can either be a source of ongoing fear or unfolding excitement.

PRACTICE
REFRAMING FAILURES

This exercise might bring up some uncomfortable feelings. If that happens for you, please stay with the discomfort as much as you can and keep yourself curious about the progress you might make by considering the following prompts and questions. First, write down three occasions in your life that you previously labeled as "failures." It doesn't really matter what kind of failures you thought they were at the time (the end of a valued relationship, something in your career that didn't turn out as planned, a fitness goal you failed to reach), just list them out as clearly as possible, including how you responded to them. Did you fall into a slump? Get back up and try again? Were you punished somehow for the failure? Second, go through each occasion and try to find at least one unexpected positive outcome that emerged as a result. For example, you might not have succeeded in making one romance work, but the breakup led to you meeting your current partner. Or being passed over for a desired promotion led you to pursue additional training, reach out to a mentor, or some other action that generated something positive for you. More often than not, what we consider failures are just necessary steps on our life path. Finally, look at each of these episodes and determine how you could have demonstrated a more curious response while they were happening. Replaying and reframing these potentially difficult moments will help you meet future challenges in more adaptive ways. When the next thing comes up that you might formerly have deemed a failure, you might instead pause and wonder, *What's the lesson here?* or *How am I going to use this opportunity to grow?*

WHERE'S THE JOY?

The above practice helped me overturn a decades-old negative mindset that would regularly lead me to self-sabotage. When I didn't perform at my peak in a competition, I would punish myself afterward with an unbelievably difficult training regimen. I would also blame myself for things I couldn't change, such as the fact that my body wasn't ideally suited to short track skating. I needed longer legs, a shorter torso, more height, and a leaner body composition. My extreme bouts of training were motivated by my anger and dissatisfaction about a physical reality that I had little to no influence over, and the negative emotions that stayed with me as a result didn't allow me to enjoy what I was doing. Eventually, I had to have a hard talk with myself and come to accept that my body wasn't going to fundamentally change, and I also wasn't going to be perfect every single time I competed. Making unreasonable demands on myself wasn't helping; in fact, it only led to me digging even deeper psychological holes that I had to fight even harder to climb my way out of.

This is part of why I'm so big on self-acceptance. Harshly criticizing yourself all the time just leads to more misery and extra obstacles between you and your goals. I had to work through the challenge of deeply accepting myself as I am, own the times I told myself I had "failed," and then try to reframe these events in more constructive ways. In short, I had to bring my curiosity to the forefront. Instead of just asking myself things like, *How can I get faster or stronger so I don't lose next time?* I was able to ask, *What am I excited about?* and *What keeps me motivated?* and *Where's the joy?* The types of questions you ask yourself make all the difference.

I tried to recover the mentality I had as a kid, when I regularly experienced the pure joy of discovery and exploration. I played every sport available to me growing up, and I had an innate ability to pick up physical skills just by watching others perform an activity. Getting better at games and sports was truly enjoyable to me, and mastering them pushed me to go even further. Unfortunately, as I grew older and entered competitive sports (eventually specializing in speed skating), my natural inclinations and drives became routinized and expected of me. Over time, I became less and less motivated by the pure fun of the sport.

Sure, it's natural to lose some of our childhood openness and wonder. But far too often it's hammered out of us. What starts as external pressure from our parents, teammates, or coaches soon becomes internalized as self-discipline or a hypercritical attitude toward ourselves. This is especially true with Olympians and other professional athletes. Most people only see our brief heroics or public defeats; they don't see the ongoing mental health issues (not to mention the physical struggles that come with injuries and recovery) that go with living with such high-stakes performance pressure. Even so, I think that all of us—even those of us on the big stage—can tap into the more curious, fun, and playful parts of ourselves. Bringing those parts online makes all the difference.

In 2006, the Winter Olympics were held in Turin, Italy. On the day I arrived, I started warming up by taking some laps inside the ice arena. It was quite cold, but I decided that I wanted to jog outside instead. I knew the officials wouldn't like it because they always want to keep track of the athletes to ensure their safety and to make sure the facility remains secure at all times. But on that day, I didn't care. I was going outside, no matter what.

IF YOU'RE NOT HAVING FUN,
IT'S ONLY A MATTER OF TIME UNTIL
YOU START SABOTAGING YOURSELF.

The sun was shining a little bit, and I felt free and energized. I remember thinking, *this* is why I do it. I committed to the highest level of athletic competition for *this* routine, *this* challenge, *this* game, and *this* playful experience. Later that day, I won the gold medal in my first event. I felt the spirit of play with me the entire time, as if I were a child again—just a kid playing a game. I think it took that moment of scoffing at authority and escaping outside to tap into that youthful attitude. Not that I endorse rule-breaking, but in some cases, it can have a positive effect that doesn't lead to any harm.

This experience helped me realize that I tend to be way more productive and successful when I take a playful approach. That's still true today and in completely different activities (the investments and businesses I'm involved with). I keep a structure and routine to my day, waking up early and making sure I exercise and eat well, but I also crack jokes, take long breaks to enjoy myself, and try to get everyone I see to smile. I try my best to cultivate a sense of freedom and those flow states in which I'm not trying too hard, but I'm still working toward my goals with a sense of effortlessness and bliss. And I also prioritize joy because if you're not having fun, it's only a matter of time until you start sabotaging yourself.

Some of the most successful people in the world speak about orienting themselves with a sense of play and curiosity, as opposed to hard-core ambition. The business magnate Warren Buffett, for example, talks about how he is much less concerned about the outcome of the game he's playing in his professional life than he is about simply enjoying it. He's known to spend most of his day reading to satisfy his curiosity about the investments he wants to make.[3] He's hit upon the formula for continuing and lasting success, which is demonstrated both by his incredible financial worth and his sense of contentment. Satisfying your curiosity continuously is a source of immense pleasure and joy, and in people like Buffett's case, it's actually integral to ongoing success.

Joy allowed me to finally balance my hyper-competitive drive with a more mature understanding of lightheartedness and play. I now know that I do my best when I'm in this state of play, but that doesn't mean it's easy. But even when things get difficult, most of the time I can remain focused and still enjoy the process, and I know I'm doing something right if I'm smiling in the face of a challenge.

CURIOUS IDENTITIES

There are countless examples in today's economy of people being forced to hard pivot and having to reach deep to find joy. One day you're following your dream as a musician, English teacher, or auto mechanic, and the next day you're out of a job and scrambling to make ends meet. I travel a lot, and I'm always meeting new people, so I'm constantly hearing about how people answer that *What now?* question I talked about in chapter 1.

CURIOSITY IS CATCHING, ESPECIALLY WHEN WE SHARE IT WITH OTHER PEOPLE.

For example, Uber and Lyft drivers regularly tell me that they didn't exactly have Uber and Lyft on their childhood list of fantasy careers. They aren't doing the work because it was their dream job; they're doing the work because it's how they're able to survive and take care of their families. It can be extremely challenging to have to make a living like that, both practically and psychologically, but most of the drivers I speak to aren't moping around complaining about how demeaning the work is. Instead, they engage their curiosity by asking me questions, engaging me in conversation, and thereby enjoying their job as much as possible. It might not be ideal, but they get to constantly learn about other people—their own struggles, experiences, and travels—and that curiosity about the living person in the back seat is often what keeps them going. They might not end up driving people around for the rest of their lives, but it pays the bills, and they're trying to make the most of it while they're at it.

I told you a little bit about my dad in chapter 2. He didn't come to the United States with a dream of cutting hair for a living. He was studying to be an accountant, when—seemingly out of the blue—he came across an opportunity to earn money by cutting people's hair, and it's a job he holds to this day. He doesn't do it because it pays outrageously well or because he necessarily enjoys the craft of it; my dad still cuts hair because it gives him a sense of purpose and engages his curiosity constantly.

In addition to being the unofficial mayor of Belltown, my dad also gets to serve as the neighborhood's unofficial (and unlicensed) psychologist. He asks his clients about their lives—their politics, relationships, careers, and so on—and gets to speak with them openly and transparently, all while giving them an excellent haircut. Being a hair stylist and salon owner isn't as much a part of my father's identity as his curiosity is. The work is just a vehicle for that.

It's not unusual for us to end up fulfilling unofficial roles for others like this. Curiosity is catching, especially when we share it with other people. Interestingly enough, years ago one of my dad's clients took an interest in me and became instrumental in my development as a curious person.

Maria was a trained journalist and extremely inquisitive by nature. Simply by recommending books to me from when I was a teen (specifically, the works of Nikos Kazantzakis, Carl Jung, and Viktor Frankl), Marie did more to further my education than any college ever could. She also mentored me in how to ask probing questions of myself and the world: *What does it mean to live a good life? How do you know if you're living well?* Whatever the topic, Maria taught me how to have introspective conversations with myself and seek my inner truth. She never provided answers because she wanted me to do the hard work of figuring it out on my own. She also supported me in my sport by encouraging my interest in optimizing every element of my physical life by trying all sorts of methods for mindfulness, diet, sleep, and energy management. Getting that encouragement, along with the advice of my coaches and peers, helped me develop routines that keep me in top shape to this day.

Because I didn't grow up with a mother, Maria filled much of that spiritual role for me, encouraging me to follow my inner voice and guiding the development of my sense of right and wrong. Earlier in the book, I limited my personal board of directors to a starting five, but Maria would easily be my sixth member of the board. Especially when it comes to my own hard pivot after I retired, Maria has been instrumental—in fact, she was the one who prodded me into going back to school. Maria was adamant that I needed more formal training in business in my post-skating life, and on her recommendation, I enrolled in an executive business course at the Wharton School of the University of Pennsylvania.

I still don't think formal education is the best fit for everyone, but Maria was right: it turned out to be exactly what I needed.

PRACTICE
GETTING CURIOUS

Maria helped me see the importance of letting my curiosity and passion drive my learning process. What do I want from life? What am I most excited about? When I'm talking to my friends, what is it that I most want to share with them? What are the activities I most look forward to? Here's your opportunity to explore your own answers to these questions. Take your notebook and draw a line down the center of the page. On the left side, list as many things in your life that you would call *amazing*–anything you want to experience more of, foster, or learn more about. You may also want to see what comes to mind when you think about the words *inspiring, special, sacred,* and *fascinating*.

A friend of mine who completed this practice included the following in his list: sunsets, hot springs, playing guitar, snowboarding, comedy nights, photography, and vintage motorcycles. All of these were invigorating and irresistible to him. What does it for you? Feel free to think back on what you most enjoyed in life when you were a kid too.

Once you've filled out that inspiring left-hand column, use the right side of the page to write down some action steps–in other words, what it would take to experience your favorite things, people, and activities more often. For example, if snowboarding is also on your list, you might write "buying a season pass" and "keeping my Saturdays free" in the right-hand column. Then, after filling out both lists, check in with how you're feeling. More excited? Eager to get started? Motivated to try out one of your stated action steps? Giving yourself emotional experiences like this will help activate your curiosity, and writing things down in this way will increase the chances that you'll end up following through with at least one thing that keeps you pumped up and excited about being alive.

On a side note, the friend I mentioned above wrote "take a course in photography" as an action step, and then he actually did it. That led to a career as an event photographer, and he's also applied his new skills to capturing beautiful sunsets, vintage motorcycle shows, and other things he loves. I can't promise you the same life-changing success from doing this practice, but I do know that your own hard pivot will benefit from trying it out. It's practices like these that will help you begin the action part of your adventure as soon as possible.

THE MOST USEFUL GIFT

There's a quote that's often attributed to Eleanor Roosevelt that goes something like, "At a child's birth, if a mother could ask a fairy godmother to endow it with the most useful gift, that gift would be curiosity."[4] I don't believe in fairy godmothers, but I'll end this chapter wishing the same gift for you.

Once you set out on your journey to reinvention, there's no way of knowing where the road is going to take you. Everybody's rabbit hole is different, but if you can remain curious when you get to the next turn in the tunnel, it will help keep you from getting bogged down when things are less than ideal. Even when you come across the inevitable obstacles or hit a dead end, curiosity is the thing that gets you looking around for creative solutions and new beginnings. In my opinion, curiosity is a much more valuable gift than formal training (although having both is probably an asset). Reinventing yourself isn't simply about strenuous effort and discipline; it's about opening your heart and mind, exploring your world with a sense of wonder, and being willing to take unconventional paths.

I strongly believe that life will show you where to go next if you're open and curious. Living this way takes a lot of letting go of habituated norms, and it also takes a lot of practice. The good news is that it's never too late to grow, to change, to follow your dreams, to take a different path. Countless new scientific studies about the neuroplasticity of our brains and nervous systems back me up here.

When I made my hard pivot into the business world, I engaged my curiosity with a lot of passive learning—reading everything I could get my hands on, listening to relevant podcasts, and questioning experts for the answers I needed. That works for a lot of people, but I'm more of a hands-on guy, so eventually I had to take the next step: I had to learn by doing.

My first foray into business happened through a friend whose family ran one of the most successful engineering firms in China. They produced rare earth minerals—vital components for all our modern electronics.

In fact, our economy simply couldn't function without rare earth minerals, so I figured it was a great place to start. Because of my Japanese heritage and American upbringing, I've always thought of myself as a sort of ambassador between East and West. I didn't know much about geology, refining minerals, or engineering, but I had a superb work ethic, and I felt confident that I could help my friend's company grow their market outside of Asia. The company saw my potential and gave me an opportunity that I turned into a job that took me to seventy countries all over the world. I traveled and spoke to hundreds of people, explaining the company's business and creating new deals. Every day I was learning by doing. And I couldn't have predicted any of it.

One day I was dropped off at a rare earth factory in the middle of Yixing, China, two hours outside of Shanghai. I was disoriented and overwhelmed. But at that point in my hard pivot, I was fairly practiced at hitting the curiosity switch, so I just followed the workers and managers around all day and asked them endless questions through my translator. I'm not sure what their experience of that day was like, but I came away newly inspired and educated. Instead of leaving the *doing* to somebody else, I had placed my curious self right in the center of the factory's activity, which helped me immensely later on when I had to know more about terms of use, the science of production and mining, the industry's economic outlook, and so on.

Nobody at that factory knew that I was an Olympic athlete, and if they did know, they didn't much seem to care. I was years behind them in terms of experience, but I knew that activating my curiosity would help me identify what strengths I brought to the table. I was determined not to be some washed-up athlete who gets in the way and pokes his nose around where it doesn't belong. I knew I could contribute in a unique way. I just had to figure out what that was.

Here, again, I have to thank my personal board of directors. Because I had trained with Doug Jowdy, I knew the benefits of calming my mind before any kind of practice (and even in the middle of a challenging task) to foster clarity and attain optimal states of mind. So when I had to learn about a new industry from the ground up, I applied what Doug taught me to accelerate my uptake and learning. In turn, that empowered me to identify the important differences between one rare earth mine and the next and to evaluate the capacities of engineers and the potential of different deposits around the world. My focus and curiosity paid off; eventually, I was put in charge of figuring out the company's competitive positioning in the market. This was a major personal achievement for me since I had been completely ignorant of the industry just months before. But my curiosity allowed me to prove my worth and make a significant contribution in record time.

Before my hard pivot, had you asked me to fill out the two columns in the "Getting Curious" practice offered a few pages back, rare earth minerals probably would be nowhere on the list. However, "learning new things," "talking to people," and "traveling the world" would be. That's just to say that sometimes we're tasked with jobs or duties outside the scope of our organic interest, and it's up to us to leverage our curiosity to find a way in.

If we discover ways to care about outcomes, we'll naturally come up with creative solutions to meet the challenges that arise. We all have friends who did poorly in school, but who are perfectly brilliant in some other way. Let's say they failed every science test they ever took, but they're an incredible dancer or they can list off hundreds of NBA stats as if it were nothing. Introduce that kid to kinesthetics or the physics of basketball, and it's likely that they'll become genuinely interested in science and learn way more than anyone ever expected.

That's the sort of Jedi mind trick you have to learn to play on yourself. If you want to dive into an entirely new field—either out of necessity or just for the hell of it—I recommend finding ways to gamify your experience. What are you already interested in that applies? Where's the door in? And, if you can't find a door, maybe you can dig a tunnel or create a magic portal. Have fun with it. There's almost always a way to get curious and make what's in front of you more interesting.

PIVOT POINTS

• Curiosity promotes a sense of exploration and pulls you out of anxious frames of mind.

- Learn from your losses, grow, and try again.
- Make curiosity your superpower.
- More often than not, self-criticism just places more obstacles in your path to reinvention.
- Focus on what makes you excited. Prioritize what brings you joy.
- When faced with difficulties, find interesting ways to bring your curiosity on board.

CHAPTER SIX

Choose Love

It's never too late to learn anything for which you
have a potential. If you want to learn to love, then
you must start the process of finding out what it is,
what qualities make up a loving person and see how
these are developed. Each person has the potential for
love. But potential is never realized without work.[1]

LEO BUSCAGLIA

s important and all-encompassing as love is as a basic
human nutrient, I haven't always been able to love others
well. I've also had trouble receiving love—from other people, but also from myself. I chalk this up to a number of factors, and
I'm sure that anyone with similar struggles could do the same. Whether
it's our childhood upbringing, the culture of our immediate community,
personal temperament, or societal messaging, love (and the essential
nourishment it brings us) isn't always easy to come by.

Growing up as the child of a single parent, I missed out on some
formative attachment experiences. Other than my dad, the only thing
I truly loved growing up was skating, which I totally dedicated myself
to, meaning that I had very little energy left over for other pursuits or
people. Due to the nature of my upbringing and my commitment to the
sport, my faculties of vulnerability, love, and empathy lagged behind
my physical prowess, strict discipline, and ability to home in and focus.
Unfortunately, that resulted in me being somewhat heartless at times, as
well as harsh, critical, and self-punishing.

I still struggle with all these things, but I've grown a lot since I was a kid—especially after retiring from skating—and I've done a lot of work to better my relationship with love. Thankfully, I've had some incredible instruction along the way. I'm now committed to understanding the gifts of love and learning how I can evolve into a more loving person. As elsewhere in this book, my hope is that by sharing some of my personal story, I can help shed some insight and even offer you some shortcuts when it comes to your own challenges.

WHAT'S LOVE GOT TO DO WITH IT?

As a competitive athlete, I was conditioned to be stoic and emotionless, to project an intimidating aura of invincibility, and to push myself to unreasonable limits in the ruthless pursuit of becoming the best in the world. Not surprisingly, anyone who's encouraged to be this way (especially from childhood) will tend to be selfish. There's no way around it. At the elite level of any sport, paying close attention to the smallest details of your training and health routines is crucial to your success, which means that most of the important things in life (romantic relationships, for example) usually take a back seat, if they're even given a space at all. If you don't prioritize your physical performance, you simply fall behind. That means all sorts of behaviors and choices that most people don't have to deal with in life. From draconian diets to steering clear of most social engagements because you have to wake up at 5:00 a.m. the next morning to train your ass off, the life of a pro athlete isn't exactly conducive to typical human concerns like friendship and love.

I can't say that it's like this for everybody who commits their life to sports, but I don't think the generalization is too much of a stretch. Anybody who truly wants to be the best in their chosen field—whether it's skating or brain surgery or chess—has to make some hard choices in life. I don't like to use the word *sacrifices* in this context because those of us who've made this kind of choice in life usually are so focused on the end goal that what we're missing out on doesn't register as it might otherwise. Personally, I didn't really notice the pain of a lot of that stuff. I didn't care about all the other fun activities I could be doing instead of training myself into a stupor, but I did feel the imbalance when it came to other people. Especially when it came to my teammates.

KINDNESS AND UNDERSTANDING HAVE A POSITIVE RELATIONSHIP WITH WINNING

You've heard the old "There is no *I* in team" cliche, but for some of us (namely, *me*), it simply isn't true. Although I've changed a lot since I was a kid, for years I could only see my teammates through my own eyes, and that gaze was nearly always hypercritical, cold, and rigid. Because I was so merciless with myself—skating through injury and pain, never taking breaks or days off, and demanding that I put peak performance above everything else in life—I treated my teammates with the same callousness and unforgiving judgment. If they came down with a cold or flu and needed to sit out, for example, I viewed them as weak and unworthy. If they talked about outside interests and relationships, I rolled my eyes and wrote them off. In essence, I viewed my teammates as replaceable *things* as opposed to friends or just normal people with normal wants, vulnerabilities, and needs. Because that's what happens when you take a win-at-all-costs approach to life.

But here's the thing: it doesn't have to be that way. Although dedicating yourself to something in life requires pristine prioritization and discipline, there's no real reason that love and empathy and compassion can't be a part of your life. In fact, it's all the more reason that you need them.

As it turns out, kindness and understanding have a positive relationship with winning. Endlessly worrying about losing and being viewed as inferior, pushing your body to cruel and unusual limits, and suffering from endless critiques (from yourself and others) has very little to do with optimal performance. Simply put, chronic anxiety, fear, and tension aren't good for you, no matter what you do in life.

I'm not saying that grit and perseverance and resilience aren't important. Clearly, they are. But the old paradigm has to go. There's way more to winning, living, and loving ourselves and others than tough love has to offer.

If your idea of bravery, for example, requires you to never be afraid (or never show it if you are), you won't actually become a person who doesn't feel fear—you simply become a person who hides it, who stuffs fear in a closet somewhere inside you where no one can hear it cry. And if you expect other people to do the same, that's what you encourage in them as well. And if that's the culture that's expected and promoted on a team (as it was when I was growing up), any conversation regarding anxiety, doubt, and dread gets turned inside, and usually in less-than-compassionate ways. We tell ourselves that we're weak. That we're not like the others. That we don't have what it takes. That we might as well quit.

Does any of that sound like it promotes true strength? Isn't there another way to go about winning?

PRACTICE
COUNTING CRITIQUES

I invite you to think about how this sort of self-harshness applies to your life. For now, don't worry so much about your expectations and judgments of others, just focus on what you unfairly demand of yourself. This isn't the time or place to fix any of these challenges; I just want you to list them out and shine some light on them. Some common examples include "I never give myself a break," "Too hard on myself when I make a mistake," and "Pay more attention to my failures than my successes." What are yours?

Love isn't an on-and-off switch. It's not something you're either born with or you're not. Love is an action; it's a practice you can develop and constantly hone. Even before I retired from skating, I was beginning to understand this, with no small help from some of the people on my personal board of directors. Over time, I learned to accept myself better, practice self-love, and free myself from the relentless internal criticism that fueled my early skating days. It took a lot of work, but eventually

I was able to be more open and communicative about my challenges with other people, too, and that changed my relationships dramatically.

I started paying better attention to their experiences, as opposed to just my thoughts about their experiences. As a result of treating myself with more compassion, I was able to listen to my teammates speak to their struggles with less judgment and more encouragement. I worked at cultivating my empathy and got better at offering suggestions that played more to their strengths than called out their weaknesses. And I was able to feel regret and more than a little guilt about how I'd treated them before, remembering their faces when I'd criticized them in the same manner I'd been criticizing myself. I had told myself it was well-intended, that it was just tough love, but the fact was that it was rarely helpful to any of us. Actually, I think that treating other people and myself that way was hurtful, especially when it came to developing essential qualities like understanding, acceptance, and love.

THE IMPRINTS OF PARENTING

I've already told you a little bit about my father—how he came to the United States with no money and very little English. It's a tribute to his upbringing that my dad was able to immigrate with only his ambition and a sense of adventure in his pockets and go on to create a successful life for himself. Having grown up in Japan, he wasn't afraid to work tremendously hard to get that.

When I was a child, my dad naturally encouraged me to succeed in the same ways he'd been parented as a child. He wanted me to be steadfast, strong, and able to achieve something extraordinary in life. He was just replicating what he was taught in his own childhood, but it was a different world back then, and Japanese child-rearing is quite different from American parenting. Especially in my father's time, Japanese parents valued achievement, obedience, and indifference to hardship in ways that most Westerners would deem cold and detrimental today.

I knew that my father was different from other dads. He was less approachable and way less expressive emotionally, at least back when I was a kid. He also pushed me harder—way harder. Even when I was injured or sick, he wouldn't let up, and the thought of me quitting anything just wasn't an option. Part of this approach, too, was simply because he was parenting alone.

In Japanese families, the role of the mother is essential when it comes to balancing the emotional impact of that strictness that often comes from the father. In general, Japanese mothers are known for being more emotionally bonded to their children, whom they see as perfect little beings. Westerners often remark at how well-behaved and calm Japanese children are, and I think that's due to this interesting combination of strictness and empathy. Well, I grew up without my mother, so one half of that equation was missing.

My dad and I fought a lot when I was growing up, especially when I was a teen, but we were aligned when it came to my skating ambitions, and that saw us through. And even though he was tough on me, I always knew he was trying to help me in the long run and that his intentions were good. Over time, my dad changed, softening with age and becoming more emotionally expressive. Nowadays, in direct contrast to the messages I received in childhood, my dad is quick to remind me to be easy on myself.

IF WE WANT TO SEE THE POTENTIAL GOOD OF OTHERS, WE MUST FIRST RECOGNIZE IT IN OURSELVES.

LOVING OTHERS, LOVING SELF

My mother's absence also left me with an abandonment wound that I built layers of emotional scar tissue around. That meant that I regularly sabotaged my romantic relationships early on before they became too serious because I was afraid that I was fated to be rejected and cast aside, just as my mother had left me. I got good at pointing the finger at my girlfriends and highlighting their imperfections—either that or I behaved so terribly that they had no choice but to break up with me. It was all just a way for me to maintain control and ensure I wouldn't get hurt again.

I also wasn't prepared to be an equal partner in those relationships because I was having such a hard time with myself. In addition to the epigraph at the start of this chapter, one of my favorite quotes from Leo Buscaglia is "To love others you must love yourself . . . You can only give to others what you have yourself."[2] To me, that's saying that if we want to see the potential good of others, we must first recognize it in ourselves, and loving yourself means developing a deep, compassionate inner dialogue. That's a process of identifying and becoming okay with the person that you've become. You have to be able to look in the mirror and say, "It's okay that I've made mistakes. It's okay that I'm inconsistent. I'm going to be honest about my fears, insecurity, doubts, self-sabotage, and hunger for love and acceptance." It took me a long time to be able to do that, and my relationships suffered because of it.

It's still a challenge today. I doubt I'm alone in struggling to extend love and understanding to myself. Looking at myself in the mirror and saying, "I love you for all that you are and all of your mistakes," seems silly and indulgent, but that's what it took to shake things up with me, foster self-love, and build up my self-confidence.

PRACTICE
RESPONDING COMPASSIONATELY

I want you to look back on the common self-critiques you listed in the last practice. Now that we've uncovered them, it's time to treat them to a helping of self-compassion and understanding. I know that this practice can bring up a lot of resistance, but that's usually because we don't know what else to do but give ourselves a hard time about everything. Bear with me and try it out. For example, if you're the type of person who always dwells on your failures, try listing out some successes as well. Then take the next step and put both your failures and successes into a new context, something like, "It's important to note my failures and learn from them. It's also important to celebrate what I got right because I deserve to know and feel the goodness that comes from accomplishment." That way, you aren't just arguing with yourself about whether or not you're good or bad, but you recognize that your positives and negatives are all just aspects of the bigger picture, and that bigger picture (you) deserves love.

Over time, I realized that I was lacking unconditional love in the form of empathy and encouragement. For that reason, even when I'd win a race—including Olympic races—I often felt empty after the initial rush wore off. Winning didn't replace what I was missing inside. Medals weren't a substitute for kindness, appreciation, and self-love.

When I retired, I went through a series of awakenings about everything inside of me that was still trying to convince me that I was unworthy of love. I was reaching that age when many of my friends were pairing off and getting married, whereas I couldn't keep anyone around long enough to even think about a long-term partnership. It began to occur to me that maybe I had something do with all those failed relationships, that the way I'd treated my girlfriends was unfair and off-putting, and that I'd acted in that way not because I was innately a bad and selfish person, but because something was off in the way I was treating myself.

Loving yourself doesn't mean ignoring your faults, insecurities, and shortcomings. It means seeing everything about yourself with love and compassion. Self-compassion and self-acceptance go together, and once I was able to experience that for myself, it wasn't as much of a challenge to love others well. I had to learn those skills, of course, and work at demonstrating that I was open enough to feel someone's pain while wishing them a sense of well-being (whereas before I had a habit of challenging them to suck it up and tough it out). I learned to make a point of regularly expressing affection and providing a safe space for people I cared about to offload their difficult feelings.

DON'T FORGET THE GOOD

One of the more obvious ways I knew things were changing for me was in how I felt about my wins in life. As I mentioned before, when I was competing, I was hyper-focused on everything I was doing wrong, brushing off my successes as if they meant nothing. It was incredibly hard, too, to receive compliments from others. At the same time I yearned for their praise and approval, I wasn't able to let myself feel the appreciation of others—that kind of attention just made me grimace and squirm. But if you can't celebrate your wins, you're only getting part of the overall picture, and if you can't find joy in your own achievements, it's a lot harder to appreciate what's going well for others.

As psychologist Rick Hanson and others have recently pointed out, it's crucial that we also recognize what's going right in life.[3] We have to relish the positive and make encouraging ourselves and others a daily practice. There's a wealth of science to back this up, hundreds of studies that illustrate how detrimental it is to simply focus on negative feedback. Guilt, fear, and anxiety aren't optimal for performance, nor are they helpful when it comes to relationships. Reviewing our victories and focusing on positive goals, however, tends to keep our focus better and promote bonding between people.

PRACTICE
REMEMBERING THE GOOD

It's easy to skip over this practice, so I really invite you to try it out for yourself. What are three good things that have happened in your life recently? How about three good qualities in the people close to you? What are three things you're most looking forward to in the coming week? Try focusing on the positive in as many ways as you can think of every day for a week or so and really let yourself feel all the good feelings (hope, happiness, joy, and so on) that come from doing so. How's it different from what you normally focus on in life? Which experience do you prefer?

LOVE IN ACTION

I used to think about love in terms of being lovable, as if it were a state or inherent quality. I thought that being worthy of love required you to be attractive, popular, or successful in some way. If I could just succeed enough, I thought, people would love me and maybe I could love myself. But that's not how it works.

As psychologist Erich Fromm writes, "Love is an activity, not a passive affect . . . love is primarily giving, not receiving."[4] When we focus on love as something we *do*, consistently, we also inspire others to love as well. Fromm's book makes the case that most of us haven't learned how to practice the art of love and we mistakenly believe that we'll be loved if we just work on ourselves hard enough. That's why we put so much energy into the pursuit of money, power, and status.

Experiencing love means enacting love. It means choosing to behave in loving ways and willfully receiving love from others. It means showing up, day after day, committed to the act and art of loving. It means expressing concern, exercising compassion, and finding ways to celebrate life's victories and triumphs. It means genuinely wanting yourself and others to be happy. I know it sounds like a lot, like maybe as much as another full-time job. But what might happen if we put as much attention on loving ourselves and others as we did on our work? What would it look like to take yourself and your loved ones that seriously?

BIANCA

These are some of the lessons I've learned from my fiancée, Bianca. She's the first woman I've really connected with deeply, and I was able to open up and be vulnerable with her because I met her at a stage of my life when I was working on some of these skills. She also had no idea what a big star I was, so that helped too. Bianca wasn't in my life when I was an Olympic athlete, so she isn't as familiar with that driven, self-centered, and ruthlessly critical side of me. And that's part of why we're together.

> LOVE IS ABOUT BEING OPEN AND FLUID
> AND PAYING ATTENTION TO OTHER PEOPLE;
> IT'S ALSO ABOUT LOVING YOURSELF.

Bianca was raised by a single parent and comes from a cross-cultural background as well. She grew up in Hong Kong, London, and Chicago with her mother—a successful business owner who pushed Bianca to excel in math and science. When it became clear that Bianca was more interested in and suited to creative pursuits, her mother relented but pushed her to become a professional pianist. So, more of the same, but different. Bianca turned out to be a gifted and successful pianist, and she earned a full ride to college to study music, but she found the program to be overly rigorous and monotonous. Seeking an outlet, she signed up for a drama class, changing her entire life as a result. Bianca loved inhabiting new characters and discovered that she had a real knack for acting. Despite intense pressure and judgment from her mom, Bianca listened to her own voice and switched her major from music to drama.

Over time, Bianca found lots of work modeling, doing print ads, and taking roles in TV commercials, and she ended up making a lot more money than she would've made as a professional pianist. Not that she was doing it for the money, but it helped with her mother, who in turn advised Bianca on her investments in real estate and her restaurant business. And all of it came to her because she decided to hard pivot early on in life and pursue what she most loved.

In addition to illustrating the importance of making those choices in life, Bianca has taught me a lot about the value of empathy and communication. In terms of empathy, I've always been amazed at how Bianca experiences real pain herself when she sees others suffering—people and animals alike. That's been so helpful for me because for years I tried to shield myself from others' pain. When my teammates would get hurt on the ice, I'd just look away and try not to show even a quiver of emotion. Being witness to Bianca's openness and resilience in the face of pain has helped me understand that it's okay, that's it's healthy and beneficial to have those feelings. It doesn't make you weaker; it actually makes you stronger and more whole.

As far as communication goes, Bianca has taught me that a rewarding relationship requires mutual understanding. We don't always have to agree, but we do need to listen to where the other partner is coming from, and that takes patience, which also takes practice. Everything worthwhile takes practice. Love is an action; it's not a static state of appreciation for some ideal love-object. Love is about being open and fluid and paying attention to other people; it's also about loving yourself. Loving Bianca well also means loving Apolo well, and both are an ongoing practice.

PRACTICE
I LOVE WHO YOU ARE

For this exercise, I want you to take a piece of paper and draw two lines down the middle of it, making three equal columns. Your first task is to list your top five qualities you imagine that other people see in you. What are the traits that make you unique? Put anything that comes up in the left-hand column.

Next, take a few minutes to look at yourself neutrally in a mirror. You're not looking for flaws, nor are you preparing for your hottest selfie. You're just trying to see yourself plainly, without any bias. Once you feel you're at that place, look into your eyes and say, out loud, "I love you for who you are," then say it again several times. With each repetition of this sentence, try to feel the love emanating from the image in the mirror. This is just one practice to help you enact self-love. Feel that unconditional acceptance and affection radiating into your mind and body.

This is the best place from which to address your shortcomings—not from harshness and self-loathing, but from kindness and love. So, if you've gotten this far, reflect on some of the things about yourself you'd like to work on. In the middle column of the paper, write down anything about yourself you'd like to change or improve, and then read that list out loud. Look at yourself in the mirror again and say, "I know that I'm imperfect, and this is just who I am today. I love myself entirely." Say it as many times as you need for the message to really sink in. Take as long as you'd like for this stage of the practice.

This is where you get to come up with the playbook. Once you've practiced self-love and *then* acknowledged what you'd like to work on, you can grab your metaphysical chisel and start tapping away. In the right-hand column, respond to each item you put down in the middle column with an action that addresses it. For example, if you put "sometimes I'm impatient with others" in the middle column, "take three deep breaths before speaking to them" might be a good solution for the right-hand column. Once you've got your list filled out, return to the mirror and read each solution aloud to yourself, but begin each statement with "I commit to doing this action out of love."

See pages 84-85 for one version of how I've done this exercise.

If you're still wondering what love has to do with it—how love applies to optimal performance, reinvention, or hard pivoting—I'll just say that love is way more powerful (and empowering) than most of us think. Love keeps us anchored to what makes life matter, as opposed to chasing metrics that rarely get us what we really want anyway. Love ties us to our purpose, and it also promotes connection to ourselves, others, and the greater world. Winning didn't do that for me, love did. Love for myself, love for Bianca, love for my father and friends, and love for this complex, endless, imperfect, and wonderful journey.

PIVOT POINTS

- Kindness and compassion are conducive to genuine success.
- Love isn't something you *have;* love is something you develop and hone.
- Begin by extending love and understanding to yourself.
- Make a joyful habit of recognizing what's going right in your life. There's almost always something to feel grateful for.
- Choose to behave lovingly toward others and to receive their appreciation and love in turn.
- Love will anchor you to your purpose.

TOP FIVE QUALITIES	AREA TO IMPROVE
KIND	BEING MORE PATIENT
GENEROUS	INCREASING EMPATHY
HONEST	STAYING FOCUSED
AUTHENTIC	CARVING OUT PROPER TIME FOR "BIG ROCK" PROJECTS
DRIVEN	SAYING "NO" MORE OFTEN

ACTION / OPPORTUNITY

TRY AN INTENTIONAL PAUSE BEFORE
STEPPING IN OR TAKING ACTION

CONSIDER "WHAT DOES THIS PERSON
NEED" OR "WHAT DO I NEED" TO OFFER
GRACE & CONNECTION WHEN NEEDED

TURN OFF NOTIFICATIONS & SET
DEVICES ASIDE DURING TIMES WHEN
MY FULL ATTENTION IS REQUIRED

ESTABLISH TWO MORNINGS EACH
WEEK TO MAKE PROGRESS ON MY
MOST MEANINGFUL ENDEAVORS

SCHEDULE NON-NEGOTIABLE DOWNTIME
IN MY CALENDAR EACH WEEK
(AND STICK WITH IT!)

CHAPTER SEVEN

Finding Your Purpose

Life's most persistent and urgent question
is, "What are you doing for others?"[1]
REVEREND DR. MARTIN LUTHER KING JR.

My dad's plan of becoming an accountant didn't work out. He was more suited to spending time with people and helping them in whatever way he could, which is why his hard pivot saw him ultimately become a hairdresser. My fiancée was a super-talented pianist who left it all behind to pursue her passion for acting. My pal Jeremy Bloom, an Olympic skier who won world championships, left the sport and was drafted into the NFL by the Philadelphia Eagles. After his stint playing pro football, Jeremy decided to pivot again and go to business school. Shortly after, he founded an enterprise software company that has raised $40 million in funding to date. Jeremy built his company essentially from nothing because he was driven by purpose, and a big part of that purpose was giving back. He started a charitable foundation that helps low-income seniors fulfill lifelong wishes.

History is full of changemakers who made similar pivots and ended up having a huge impact in their fields. Ellen DeGeneres started out as a paralegal. Stephen King was a school janitor who only wrote stories during his off hours. Walt Disney was fired from his first position as a newspaper editor because his boss thought he lacked creativity. Pope Francis was once a bouncer at a nightclub in Buenos Aires. It often takes a hard pivot or two to make dreams come true, but pivots are just arbitrary turns unless they have purpose.

WHAT PURPOSE MEANS

I want to define *purpose* as your ultimate and unwavering source of motivation that overrides any mood, setback, or hardship you might be encountering in the moment. Your purpose is your ultimate answer to the question *Why?* Across all the changes and challenges in your life, your purpose is your North Star that guides what goals you pursue and how you show up. When you look back at your life and all the things you accomplished, your purpose will be that which provided an undying source of meaning for you. It's the thing you stood and fought for, over and over.

We all have short-term desires that come and go. Maybe you want to earn a bonus at work, get the latest iPhone or techno gadget, or take a long vacation abroad. Any of these might fulfill you for a while, but the shine wears off after a while, and before you know it, you're chasing the next short-term thing that won't ever provide you with much long-term significance.

Purpose is different. Purpose stays with you; it orients you through life. Your purpose might evolve as you age and grow, but it will typically stay the same for years at a time, and it will usually endure for as long as you remain committed to it. When you ground your life in your purpose, inspiration and motivation aren't so hard to come by. We all know people who live with obvious purpose. They've dedicated their lives to what they find meaningful, and they've sustained their efforts to it over time. They're clear about what they want to accomplish, why it matters to them, and who it actually helps.

Most people have a hard time finding purpose and remaining connected to it. There are plenty of good reasons why this is true—cultural influences, family messaging, financial hardships, social injustices of all sorts—but the fact is that far too many people who are capable of connecting to their purpose and living from that space don't do so. Especially in the United States, people seem to drift, dream, and dabble through life, never applying themselves consistently to one aim. They may pursue their own enjoyment, jumping from interest to interest, but the choices they make don't add up to inspire change or impact. They spend most of their lives chasing the next horizon, the next thrill or distraction.

This has never been more true than in today's digital age. People are increasingly fixated on the short bursts of pleasure and ego boosts they get from instant communication and social media. They try to emulate influencers and get tossed around by envy, imitating what they think other people are doing to "win" at life instead of searching inside for what they really want. It's way too easy to get caught up in marketed shortcuts to fame and fortune—game shows, reality TV, playing the lottery, YouTube, TikTok, and so on. Far too often, this is what passes for success in our culture; all the while there's a widening economic gap between rich and poor in the modern world.

Whereas once we saw virtue in sustained effort, commitment, and profound reflection, nowadays we seem to only celebrate quick and flashy success. We're sold this idea that it's just as possible (if not more so) to wake up famous and wealthy one day by finding the right hook or platform. Today's cultural heroes aren't known because they're charitable, hardworking, or wise; they're simply valued for their looks, material possessions, or their fleeting romantic relationships to other stars.

ANOTHER WAY

Other than token gestures, what's missing from the publicized lives of influencers is a genuine concern for others. For the people I most look up to, other-centered purpose plays a starring role in their overall focus. It fuels them with the energy of connection, and that transcends shallow wins to give them heartfelt satisfaction when they meet their goals, rather than the temporary buzz that comes from buying the latest toy or gaining another thousand followers. Additionally, grounding their concern in the well-being of others provides them the grit they need to overcome obstacles.

WE'RE BIOLOGICALLY WIRED TO CARE ABOUT AND ACT ON THE BEHALF OF OTHER PEOPLE.

When Dr. Martin Luther King Jr. asked, "What are you doing for others?" I think he was trying to get people to remember what's most important in life. It's not so much an issue of morality or altruism; the question of how we contribute to something greater than ourselves has everything to do with our identity, happiness, and well-being. Understanding that we're all interconnected is what sustains us. More than our individual achievements, it's what makes life worth living.

For the longest time, we've been told quite the opposite. Whether from science or religion, we've been taught that people are basically selfish and aggressive, and that cooperation and generosity mostly happen only when we're steered in that direction by authorities or some higher power. Yet studies show that despite our evident self-interest as a species, we also have an equally vital interest in others. In fact, we're biologically wired to care about and act on behalf of other people. We humans evolved to look out for the welfare of our group, just like so many other cooperative species—bees, birds, bats, rats, chimpanzees, trees, mycelial networks . . . all of these and many others have evolved to survive and thrive with generosity and resource sharing built into their behavior.

No surprise, then, that when researchers look into the most important elements of a meaningful life across a wide spectrum of people, they find that contributing to others or to something beyond their individual lives is critical. When people act generously, their brain chemistry changes in ways that make them feel better. And if workers directly witness the positive benefit of their work on others, they tend to perform better and experience more satisfaction. In the restaurant industry, for example, if the chef has a view of the dining area and can see the people she's cooking for, service tends to be faster and the customer's satisfaction goes up significantly as well. There's a similar effect in other professions if the person doing the work can tap into the emotions and responses of the people they're serving. This means that we all have the power to become more motivated and effective in whatever work we do, simply by connecting with the people who benefit.

PRACTICE
WHO BENEFITS?
Take a moment and think about a specific person who benefits from what you do. It could be one of your coworkers, a family member, a customer, or somebody far away on a remote island in the Pacific you'll

never see. Once you have that person in mind, imagine them in the moment that they receive whatever you did or gave them. Is it your daughter at school, opening up her lunch that you packed with love that morning? Is it your boss who knows that your work led to a revenue increase? Is it that client you saw last week who wrote to tell you how much they appreciated your advice? Maybe it's the customer whose bag you carried out to their car after checkout. Tune in to how that person responds to you and your work. Tangibly visualize how your work matters to others, no matter how small or laden with drudgery it may feel to you.

Even if you're currently stuck in a job you hate, you can usually find some way that your work positively influences the well-being of others. Reminding yourself of this healthy connection can bring more enjoyment or satisfaction to what you do, even if you're in the middle of looking for another job or life path. Even if we're not aware of it, most of us are already contributing a great deal to others. Simply asking yourself, *What do I contribute?* or *What more can I do?* is often enough to ground you in some purpose, perhaps even of the sort that you can orient your life around. It comes back to that relentless curiosity I talked about in chapter 5.

Determining your purpose takes asking important questions that might take some reflection time to answer. What is it that only you can do? What are you here to do right now? Start with one question, take your time to answer it thoroughly, and go from there. Over time, more questions will follow to prompt you toward your purpose, but I want to emphasize the importance of getting started. If you don't already know your purpose, I don't recommend putting off figuring it out.

As Viktor Frankl states in *Man's Search for Meaning*, our need for purpose is as important to our psychological growth as eating is to our biological growth.[2] Purpose is nutrition for your mind and soul. Studies show that people who have a high level of meaning and purpose in their life enjoy better mental health, better sleep, less pain and stress, and overall longer lives than control groups.[3]

IKIGAI

I've spent a lot of time in Japan, where life spans are notably longer than they are in the West. Japanese women live about eighty-seven years on average, whereas the life expectancy of Japanese men is about eighty-one. In the US, those numbers are substantially lower, with women living to around eighty and men to seventy-five on average. Additionally, Japanese people in general have much lower rates of cancer and cardiovascular disease. Clearly, they're doing something different, and it's more than just eating a lot of sushi.

The increased longevity and better health of Japanese people has been attributed by some to *ikigai*—an old concept recently "discovered" by a number of Westerners who have written several books on the subject. The term roughly translates to "life value" or "life worth," although sometimes you'll see it rendered as "the reason for getting up in the morning." Although ikigai has been somewhat misunderstood and co-opted in Western terms (making ikigai more about maxing out everything in life—work, productivity, money, joy, and so forth), I still think there's a lot of value to be had in some of these presentations, and my hope is that you'll find some use here without mistaking the innovation for the genuine article. I just want you to be aware that ikigai is a lot more nuanced than the purpose diagram you'll find below. Ikigai also shouldn't be anyone's excuse for finding ways to work harder, longer, or faster.

THE WORLD IS FILLED WITH
CONTRADICTORY DEMANDS,
UNREASONABLE EXPECTATIONS, AND
OUTDATED MESSAGES THAT DON'T ALWAYS
HAVE OUR BEST INTERESTS IN MIND.

Ikigai is a personal thing. Yours is necessarily different from mine, and no one's ikigai is handed down to them by anyone else. What makes each of us get up in the morning and have hope for the future depends on multiple factors, and all of us are subject to losing touch with our life's purpose from time to time. For that reason, reflection and ikigai go hand in hand.

Sometimes it takes slowing down, breathing deeply, and asking myself some hard questions to remember my ikigai. Conversely, thinking about my ikigai—grounding myself in my purpose—makes reflection and deceleration come more naturally. In today's world, it's all too easy to continuously look forward, zoom in on the details of the moment, and respond to the pressures of life by speeding up. It takes the opposite of that to remember your truth and to consciously recenter into your long-term goals. Slowing down and seeing the bigger picture is a skill that most of us can practice and develop because the world is filled with contradictory demands, unreasonable expectations, and outdated messages that don't always have our best interests in mind.

As I'm writing this, the 2020 Summer Olympics (due to COVID-19, held in July and August of 2021) provide a telling example of how the world of expectations—at least for top-tier athletes—has changed since I last competed: Simone Biles, a top gymnastics contender, removed herself from four out of five finals events. As I've mentioned before, when I was skating and had a bad day or somehow felt challenged either physically or psychologically, it would have been unthinkable to sit out of a competition or training session. The pressure to push through pain, even at the expense of our long-term well-being, was simply too great. Especially when the Olympics came around, when I felt even more pressure to keep going no matter what, because I felt that the entire citizenry of the United States was counting on me to carry the flag and represent them with as many gold medals as I could possibly earn.

There's so much of that I'd never change. I absolutely loved skating on the big stage, and I dedicated grueling years to earn each and every win, no matter who was watching. That being said, it would have been so much healthier for me and my fellow athletes had we lived in a time when it was possible to do what Simone Biles did at the 2020 Summer Olympics.

In my day, we just didn't have a way to acceptably communicate our true needs, so we stoically paraded forward, even when we were suffering physically or mentally, and many of us were the worse for it. My life and success as a speed skater were more fueled by the desire to achieve a near unreachable level of success and to meet the demanding expectations placed on me by others, rather than a personal sense of well-being, service, satisfaction, and purpose.

Simone Biles removing herself from competition to focus on her own well-being would have been inconceivable when I was skating. Her decision represents some necessary changes in sport, but it also reveals one athlete's commitment to her own ikigai. Instead of performing for others exclusively—and doing so at her own expense—Biles chose to prioritize herself, the bigger picture, and the impact she knew she could make in the coming years. To have an Olympic superstar and arguably the greatest gymnast ever (hands down) publicly choose—amidst immense pressure and predictable criticism—to focus on her own well-being is a much wider hard pivot that I hope will change the competitive community for years to come.

Does it matter if Simone Biles got to the podium? Or is it more important that she demonstrate to sports fans and young athletes around the world what they should expect from champions when they face very human challenges? Biles showed that she was willing to put her whole life's work and yet even more accolades aside because she valued her mental and physical safety more. Although her actions are still controversial to some, I believe that in the coming decades, most of us will look back at what Biles did as a feat of personal strength and a pivotal moment in the world of sports.

PRACTICE
DIAGRAMMING YOUR PURPOSE

You may already have a sense of what your ikigai is, or you may be curious to discover it. We're going to explore one example of a Venn diagram that maps out three key elements of your life's purpose: what you're good at, what you love, and what the world needs. And if you're using this exercise to inform your professional hard pivot, you can also include what you can get paid for as a fourth (optional) circle.

Take out your notebook or a piece of paper and draw this diagram, with either three or four circles, depending on where you stand in your professional life. Insert your own answers into each part of the circles, including the overlapping sections. Once you've spent as long

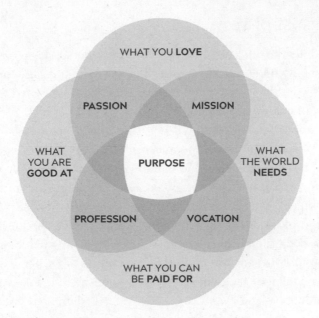

as you need to make notes, try to narrow down your ideas into one comprehensive phrase that brings it all together. Ideally, that phrase will tell you a lot about your purpose. Finally, write down a few ideas about how you could take some direct actions to live this purpose. What comes to mind?

PRACTICE
LOOKING BACK

Here's a different angle to finding your purpose: Imagine that you're at the end of a long and fulfilling life. You've accomplished just about everything you set out to do, made your best effort throughout it all, and acted with curiosity and compassion, loving others and yourself well. Upon reflection, what would you describe as your life legacy? If your admirers were going to give you a lifetime achievement award, what would it be for? What would you be most proud of accomplishing? Spend some time journaling on these questions and others you can think of and see if it helps you clarify more about your purpose today.

THE PURPOSE OF SERVICE

Take a moment to think about people you know, personally or otherwise, who exemplify finding their purpose and applying their life to fulfilling it. Chances are that some (if not many) of them have devoted their lives to service in one way or another.

Think about Jane Goodall, the world-famous primatologist who has lived her purpose for most of her (currently) eighty-seven years.[4] From an early age, she was passionate about animals, especially primates. When she was in her early twenties, Goodall contacted anthropologist Louis Leakey about studying present-day great apes in order to understand more about early humans. Leakey loved the idea, and he helped Goodall establish a lifelong study that began with chimpanzees in the Gombe Stream National Park in Tanzania. As her work went public, Goodall took the opportunity to become an outspoken advocate for these animals and eventually many other endangered creatures as well. She is single-handedly responsible for many conservation efforts around the world to protect wildlife and safeguard their habitats. Talk about someone fulfilling their life's purpose!

My hard pivot hasn't just been about investments and new businesses; part of my ikigai, too, has to do with helping others. One of the ways I do that is through the Special Olympics, the worldwide athletic competition for folks with different disabilities that helps them discover new strengths, skills, friends, community, and much more. At the big event, which happens every two years, athletes compete with similar protocols to the Olympics—they work with coaches, unite with a team, and enjoy the thrill of testing their abilities. They're scored differently, but they still compete and earn medals, and just as in life, not everyone gets one. That means that these athletes also get to learn the same powerful life lessons I and my fellow Olympians learned about performance, failure, effort, resilience, and composure under pressure. Additionally, because this demographic is often underserved with basic health and well-being services, they also get access to quality doctors, dentists, and medical technicians at the event. I remember one deaf competitor who'd never been fitted with a hearing aid—the Special Olympics made sure he received one, which allowed him to hear his coach's voice for the very first time. People who have researched the impact the Special

Olympics has on participants have found notable increases in social competence and more positive self-perception than those found in nonparticipants. It's truly a special event that transforms lives.

For the past decade, I've traveled all over Asia to support these athletes and their programs, meeting wonderful people who have touched my heart. When I speak to them—whether amping them up before their events or helping them make sense of how they and their teammates perform—I truly enjoy sharing some of my toolkit with them to help them develop their own voice and approach to sport. Before they compete, I always remind them to enjoy this moment: to smile, to remember why they compete in the first place, and to play! After the games, I typically share thoughts about managing emotions if they didn't get the results they were hoping for, and we talk about how hard they work, how they tried to do their best, and some of what they can learn from the experience. In short, these are the very messages I wished I had heard more frequently when I was competing.

Of course, helping others isn't unidirectional. Being with these athletes has taught me more than I ever expected about being open, vulnerable, compassionate, expressive, and pure of heart. One of the things I love most about the people I meet in the Special Olympics is their radical authenticity—when they're happy, they're really happy, and they aren't afraid to express it. It's the same when they're disappointed or sad. These athletes will sing, dance, and laugh whenever they feel like it, and they don't care how they look or what others think. That's so different from the world that most of us inhabit, with our constant concern about fitting in, being cool, behaving with restraint, and posing for the perfect selfie. I'm as guilty of that as anyone. With their pure love of their sport and their remarkable friendships (supporting each other through good times and bad with compassionate, caring responses), they remind me of what matters most in life, especially that it's absolutely okay to be yourself.

I met one of these friends—Jose—at a speed-skating invitational I hosted in Salt Lake City in 2015. We bonded right away because Jose is so straightforward and relentless. He says exactly what's on his mind, gives hugs without a second thought, and isn't afraid to rattle off his accomplishments in the Special Olympics. But he's also quick to tell you about his friends and all their special strengths and interests.

Jose and I still talk regularly. Even though we come from such different worlds, I feel that we're true friends and that we both bring genuine joy to each other's lives.

Friends like Jose remind me that helping others isn't just about them. Initially, I thought about my work with the Special Olympics as something I was doing for other people—giving them my free time for charity. Of course, that's not what it actually feels like. In fact, these athletes have given me so much that the exchange doesn't feel even, but maybe that's the point of service. When part of our purpose involves helping others (especially helping others connect to *their* purpose), it's a lot easier to understand that we're all connected—that my happiness and theirs go together. I can forget that from time to time, but it's actually not that hard to remember when I'm grounded in my purpose.

DEALING WITH DOUBT

I don't want to make it sound like I found my purpose right out of the gate and have spent every waking moment since then fulfilling it. I'm regularly off my game, unfocused, or just full of doubt. But at this point in my life, I understand that's all part of the journey and that doubt is just an occasional aspect of a bigger picture. In my opinion, it's normal to experience doubt from time to time; it's only when you let doubt control you that it's a problem.

One kind of doubt is what psychologists have termed *imposter phenomenon* or *imposter syndrome,* and research suggests that up to 82 percent of those studied feel like imposters at some point in their lives.[5] Imposter syndrome can be described as the feeling that you aren't up to snuff—that you've been entrusted with a task you aren't qualified to take on or promoted to a position you don't deserve. It's taking doubt one step further: you're having trouble believing in yourself, so you start thinking there's some external proof why you should. Not only that, but that other people are aware of your shortcomings or soon will be—it's just a matter of time until your secret comes to light: you're a phony, a fraud, an imposter who's just pretending to know something. Feeling this way makes it almost impossible to appreciate your successes, and you convince yourself that anything good that happens is merely on account of chance or luck. Feeling like an imposter means living in fear, mostly of being exposed. That also tends to mean shutting yourself off from others, especially when it comes to asking for help.

Sounds miserable, right? I'm depicting this kind of doubt in extreme terms, but it can also be more insidious and subtle. Especially when you embark on a new endeavor, it's common to experience doubt and feel like an imposter. I'm telling you this here in case you're actively pursuing rein-vention. Even though your hard pivot doesn't mean leaving everything behind, reinventing yourself can feel entirely new and often disorienting. In short, your new identity doesn't feel "real" yet. It can even feel inauthentic.

Be wary of this on your journey. Like I said, doubt is just part of it. But watch out for pervasive messages like the ones described above: that you aren't good enough, that you don't deserve what you've earned, that you don't belong, that you're bound to fail and be found out for the imposter you are. If you convince yourself repeatedly that everyone else in the room is without a doubt more qualified and smarter and more prepared than you are, chances are you'll find evi-dence to support that theory.

When I first started out on my hard pivot, I had to deal with nag-ging voices in my head all the time. Whenever I walked into a meeting of professionals, whether they were investors or bankers or engineers, I struggled with feeling like an imposter, and I just assumed that's how they viewed me too. I'd psych myself out so bad that I'd feel the butter-flies in my stomach morph into angry dragons chewing me up from the inside, but I had no other option but to deliver my presentation and take part in the conversation the best I could.

Over time, the doubt began to clear, and confidence slowly started taking its place. It didn't take long to see that very few people knew everything there was to know about all aspects of a given industry and that each of us at the table was merely human and limited in perspective based on our individual experiences. I was coming at things at different angles than they were, but that often meant that I had valuable insights. Gradually, the negative voices in my head dissipated, and I could focus more on the micro-wins I was achieving. Whatever small steps I could take to gain more confidence, I considered progress.

*ONCE YOU FEEL MORE
COMFORTABLE WITH WHO YOU ARE,
YOUR STRENGTHS AND ABILITIES
TEND TO SHINE THROUGH.*

Even so, I still occasionally doubt myself and feel like an imposter. But I've learned that it helps to admit when I'm lost, confused, or naive and also to not expect that I be an expert in everything. I still know very little about coding, infrastructure, and digital finance, for example, and that's okay. I'm always willing to learn, and I know my strengths: I'm more than capable of putting the time and energy in. I'm a hard worker, and that goes a long way to countering doubt.

It's key to understand what your expectations are. When I was competing, I lived under the constant pressure of unreasonable presumptions about what I should attain on a regular basis and what others expected me to do as well. Unfortunately, I applied the same irrational expectations to my entry into the world of business: I simply didn't see why I couldn't get up to speed on certain topics overnight and match my colleagues who had spent months or longer preparing their presentations and analyses. No wonder I felt like I wasn't ready! If you ask too much of yourself, get ready to fail—a lot. But if you can rid yourself of the burden of being somebody you aren't or knowing something you simply can't know (at least not yet), self-doubt won't bother you nearly as much, and the end result is liberating. As a big plus, once you feel more comfortable with who you are, your strengths and abilities tend to shine through.

PRACTICE
MINDFUL OF MASTERY
One important distinction between someone who feels like an imposter and someone who doesn't is how they respond to challenges and obstacles. Sometimes a little reframing of your thoughts will make all the difference.

We're all masters in multiple things. At one point in our infancy, for example, none of us could walk, and we toppled over dozens or hundreds of times before we eventually got it right. As adults, walking is something that most of us can do literally in our sleep or while awake and chewing gum and thinking about ten different things at once. We might forget that walking is a complex set of skills that required mastery at some point, but that doesn't make it any less so. Driving, riding a bicycle, typing efficiently, using a smartphone, learning to read and speak . . . it's the same for all of these. And I bet it's rare that you're overcome with doubt regarding these actions anymore. You just do them without thinking twice about it.

Children can certainly get frustrated when they're learning a new skill, but they don't tend to beat themselves up about it and treat themselves like imposters for even trying. They simply make the mistakes that come with being a beginner and keep trying until they get it right. That's just what it's like when you're mastering something, and doubt isn't exactly helpful to the process.

This practice is for any of you who are trying something new in life, whether it has to do with your reinvention or not. Whether it's a new computer program at work, foreign language, or complex progression in that piano piece you're learning to play, note any doubts or discouragements that come up for you. What expectations do you have for yourself? What do you think others expect of you? How reasonable are they? Do any of those beliefs take into account the fact that you haven't yet mastered the new lesson or skill? As a master of much in life, you can tap into your own experience and remind yourself that mistakes are unavoidable and, in fact, are often necessary to learning, improving, and becoming proficient at anything.

You might currently make an incredibly delicious omelet, but there was a time when you weren't all that talented at cracking eggs, and even now you probably drop a piece of eggshell or two into the bowl on occasion. How do you respond when this happens? Do you berate yourself and decide you're a breakfast-making imposter? Probably not. You simply deal with the obstacle and keep going because that's part of what it means to be a master.

Where can you apply this in your life right now? Like I've said a couple of times earlier in the book, even when we hard pivot, we don't leave everything behind. Be sure to leverage the lessons of your hard-won mastery the next time doubt comes to visit. Have a compassionate conversation with yourself about what's reasonable to expect, what isn't, and what you might learn from your mistakes along the way.

DO YOUR BEST

In the end, whether or not other people have expectations about you isn't nearly as important as how you feel inside about your own effort. That's why I recommend asking yourself, and regularly, *What do I need to do right now to feel like I'm doing my best?* Even without knowing what other people think about you, you can still build the confidence that makes you feel like you're nailing it. Whether you win the race, get the job, receive the promotion, or get high-fived by the other people in the room, you can still know that you're doing your best.

I don't want to diminish the natural desire to want the approval or praise of others; I just want to encourage you to put more energy into what matters most. The less you rely on external approval, the easier it is to follow your own guidance and become more confident and capable over time. At the end of the day, you don't have a lot of say in what other people think about you. Your true power lies in what you think about yourself. Just remember that failure is natural, that you can always learn from your mistakes, and that it's always better to put your attention on your effort rather than your results.

When you start to get the creeping feeling that everyone knows more than you do, check yourself. The nagging voice of your inner critic will definitely show up from time to time—sometimes you might even hear a whole cast of naysayers within you, each of them more convincing than the last. Don't trouble yourself so much with arguing with them—it won't do a lot of good. Instead of trying to make doubt go away, simply focus on doing your best and learning as you go.

Nobody starts at the top of the Olympic podium. It takes many, many iterations and wins and losses and failures and shortcomings and stumbles. It's okay to have imposter moments, but don't get suckered into having an imposter life. Remind yourself that it's all a journey and that you're willing to undergo transformation and travel into unknown lands for what matters most: your purpose. Knowing your purpose and doing your very best to live it is the one superpower that will see you through, no matter what.

PIVOT POINTS

- Knowing your purpose will help keep you on track and remind you how to show up.
- Your purpose serves as your North Star, although its nature and position can change in your life over time.
- Helping others is a reliable way to foster happiness, meaning, and a sense of well-being.
- Find your ikigai, but don't use ikigai just as an excuse to work harder, faster, or longer.
- Most of us feel like imposters from time to time. Admit your limitations, ask for help, and focus on doing your best.

CHAPTER EIGHT

The Five Golden Principles

As we express our gratitude, we must never
forget that the highest appreciation is not
to utter words but to live by them.[1]
PRESIDENT JOHN F. KENNEDY

Throughout this book we have explored various strategies and approaches to help you with your own reinvention, among them creating self-inventories, identifying your support team (your personal board of directors or starting five), learning how to deal with negativity and cultivating belief in yourself, firing up your curiosity, engaging love for yourself and others, and discovering your purpose. If you've committed yourself to the practices I've suggested, you probably have a notebook or stack of loose paper full of thoughts, charts, lists, and so on. This is where we put it all together and circle back to the opening of the book. Here's where we apply all that hard work to the Five Golden Principles I mentioned in the introduction: gratitude, giving, grit, gearing up, and going.

GRATITUDE

The reason that gratitude comes first is because I think it's hands down the most effective way to recondition our minds away from habitual negativity and mental defeat. Expressing gratitude as a daily practice helps us maintain perspective, cultivate empathy, and alleviate stress, and I'm not just saying that from personal experience. Consider these jaw-dropping stats: When study subjects kept gratitude journals for several weeks, they were found to be 25 percent happier than people who did not journal about what they were thankful for during the same period. Not only that, but gratitude journaling led folks to enjoy an extra half-hour of sleep and 33 percent more time exercising.[2] I can't think of too many things as simple and straightforward that could generate such a profound effect on human behavior. There are also social benefits to practicing gratitude—it increases feelings of connectedness, which leads to healthier relationships and more acts of kindness. Scientists have also quantified that people who prioritize gratitude are way more likely to be satisfied with their lives, and they experience higher levels of heart-warming emotions like joy, enthusiasm, love, and happiness. Furthermore, they develop a natural immunity to the harmful effects of envy, greed, and resentment. As a result, they can handle daily stressors without becoming unbalanced, they recover more quickly from setbacks and illness, and they are generally more physically healthy.[3]

JOURNALING WHAT YOU'RE GRATEFUL FOR WILL HELP YOU ESTABLISH A LIFE-AFFIRMING APPROACH TO THE WORLD.

Of course, turning gratitude from an occasional behavior to a regular way of life is easier said than done. The choice to say thank you to all the good life brings you doesn't come without sustained, persistent effort, but it's simple enough to get started (as I illustrated when I talked about my morning practice in chapter 3). In my experience, it's best to start small, build your gratitude muscles, and then go from there. For example, instead of searching for something profound or world-shattering to be thankful for, it's totally fine to express gratitude for a delicious cup of coffee, not being late for work, dry socks, healthy children, or the fact that you'll get to watch your favorite show on Netflix later tonight. As I'll mention later on, the most important thing is that you find a way to get started and just do it.

Gratitude truly primes my mind to remain calm, collected, and present throughout whatever happens to me next, and doing my gratitude practice every single morning (or most mornings) helps me notice moments of actual contentment during the day, which means my focus becomes less centered on negative thoughts and experiences. Of course, the benefits don't last forever, which is why I have to repeat the practice daily. Like everyone else, I get up every morning to face a world that's mostly beyond my control, but I know if I can approach the day feeling thankful, I'm probably going to make the most of it.

It also helps to write it down. Like I mentioned with one of the other practices in chapter 3, journaling what you're grateful for will help you establish a life-affirming approach to the world. As the gratitude expert Robert Emmons writes, "Writing helps to organize thoughts, facilitate integration, and helps you accept your own experiences and put them in context."[4] In my experience, journaling does all this and more.

I know it might sound a little nuts, but you can even practice being grateful for all of the difficulties and problems you face. When you look back at the challenges you've overcome in life, aren't you usually able to identify some benefit from them? Perhaps they helped you gain more emotional resilience, physical strength or endurance, or patience and perspective as the result of suffering through hard times. Be grateful for those improvements in your character and try to apply that wisdom to anything you're experiencing now that's hard, especially the challenges you may be currently facing during your reinvention. It's going to give you an unexpected edge later on, I promise.

Contrast that approach to difficulty with the widespread sense of entitlement, which, in my opinion, has become all too common in today's society. We all know ungrateful folks (maybe even ourselves at times) who express an air of self-importance and who seem to always seek ease and admiration. Some of these people are totally self-absorbed—even narcissistic—and it's rare for them to express any amount of empathy for others. Then there are just the people who feel entitled to all the good things in life without working hard to earn them. They walk around believing they're owed a huge debt, and if something goes wrong for them, they play the victim to anyone who'll listen. I'm not talking about *actual* victims who *do deserve* assistance and retribution and justice; I'm talking about people who consistently don't believe that their actions or beliefs have anything to do with whatever they're suffering. It's always someone else's fault. Something other than them is always the cause.

For people caught up in this type of thinking, finding something to be thankful for is nearly impossible. Their compass is almost stuck in the direction of lack. Maybe all of us have a little bit of that in us. If so, it's all the more reason to fix that compass and make sure it points toward gratitude—true gratitude. If you pay attention to what's going right for you and if you *make a practice of recognizing* what's going right for you, it goes a lot further than you might think.

Did you get a good night's sleep? Be grateful. Did you have enough food to eat yesterday? Acknowledge that pretty important fact and say thanks. Do you have at least one good-enough friend in the world? Well, that's something to celebrate. Start small, write it all down, and go from there, thankful for every small step.

PRACTICE
RADICALLY THANKFUL

If you tried out the gratitude practice in chapter 3, I invite you to take it one step further. Either commit to doing it for a given period (I recommend every day for at least three or four weeks) or try what I suggested a few paragraphs back: think about some of the challenges you're currently experiencing and find a way to express gratitude for them. For example, there might be somebody new at work who really gets your goat. Be thankful that they're helping you build your patience and compassion. Or maybe you've been training really hard and struggling to meet a quantifiable personal goal—a target body weight, for example, or two more servings of vegetables each day. See if you can find a silver lining in the struggle. "I made this goal because I decided it was good for me," for example, "and these challenges will make the process and reward even more worthwhile." Whatever it is, try being thankful for the hard things for a while, and see how your approach to (and experience of) future challenges changes as a result.

For whatever reason, sometimes it can be hard to feel thankful about anything that's going on in your life. Believe me, I know. When that happens (and it probably will from time to time), I suggest thinking about other people and the challenges they've faced and overcome. For me, thinking about my father's struggles as an immigrant and his quest to raise me as a solo parent while also thriving as an individual fills me with awe and makes me grateful. Thinking about my friends in the Special Olympics usually does the trick too. I remember how much happiness they bring me and other people, but I also think about all they have to deal with in life—challenges I'll never know. And if I really need a reminder of how good I have it, I just remember the kids I've visited in children's hospitals around the world because nothing puts your life in perspective quite like spending time with an eight-year-old cancer patient who just wants to go home, spend time with their friends, play outside, and do normal kid stuff without tubes in their bodies and medicines that make them feel nauseous and weird. If I just stop and remember these kids and countless others who are fighting heroic battles day in and day out, finding something to be thankful for isn't all that hard.

Gratitude makes all the difference. And if you take only one thing away from this book, I hope it's the practice of feeling grateful and saying thanks.

GIVING

Becoming a more grateful person primes you to be more generous with yourself and others. If you train your mind to focus on abundance, it's easier to feel like you have the energy and resources to help others. In the last chapter, I talked quite a bit about the importance and benefit of cultivating an other-centered purpose. Most people yearn to know they're having some positive effect on others—our giving helps them, of course, but it also lights up the pleasure and reward centers in our brains, making sure we feel the benefits of our generosity long after we've helped others. Whether you're a farmworker, teacher, chef, actor, or volunteer, your life satisfaction is going to improve when you know that what you're doing actually helps someone.

Again, I'm not just talking about helping out of some sense of obligation or moral imperative. We humans *need* to give. It's a drive that brings us physiological benefits and helps society cohere. In addition, when we give selflessly of our time, attention, and resources, it's easier to transcend our self-centeredness and the suffering that comes from a

me-first attitude. Without having to actively seek recognition or valida-
tion, giving provides a powerful pathway to personal fulfillment. These
acts of kindness create a spiral of benefit, in which gratitude leads to
generosity, which leads to happiness, which increases our ability to pursue our goals and achieve our purpose.

Years ago, I was invited to meet with kids at a public school on the
south side of Chicago. Five other schools in the area had closed due to
lack of funding, and this was the last school standing. The building just
happened to be on the top of a hill with a fabulous view of the urban sky-
line. When I entered the school, I could tell right away why this one was
still open: the principal was an energetic, fun, and giving guy who had
that special way with children. He told me that on the first day of school
he liked to take the kids up to the top of the hill and have them look
down below and tell him what they saw. Typical answers were things
like, "That's the liquor store by my house," "My cousin got shot on that
corner," and "Over there is where they sell drugs." None of the kids mentioned anything about the beautiful city shining right before them.

To the principal, it didn't matter if the kids had the fewest resources
or the worst trauma and poorest prospects for the future. I could see
that many of them were already so hardened to life, even at the age
of nine, but the principal knew he could break through their walls of
self-protection and disappointment in what life had dealt them. He
could help them see that despite everything, they possessed something special inside. They didn't have to walk in the same footsteps
as their predecessors, but they could work hard to attain something
extraordinary in life. They just had to believe it. For him, it started
with showing them the world beyond the only one they knew. It was
an inspiring visit, to say the least.

Quite often, we guard our time and resources, imagining that the
more we give to others, the less we have for ourselves. This can certainly
be true sometimes. But at the same time while we should be wary of
giving too much or being taken advantage of by others, it doesn't have
to stop our acts of generosity altogether. Psychologist Adam Grant says
that "Selfless giving, in the absence of self-preservation instincts, easily
becomes overwhelming."[5] He advises that rather than react by becoming more selfish, we can instead become "otherish," which he describes

as being willing to give more than you receive, all while keeping your own interests your top priority.

PRACTICE
GENEROSITY IN ACTION

In the last chapter, I asked you to imagine someone who is positively impacted by you, envisioning how even something that seems small or insignificant to you could actually be of genuine benefit to others. I want to invite you now to take the next step and think about someone who's currently in need–a family member, friend, coworker, neighbor, stranger, or anyone else you can think of. List three or four of them, as well as what they could use to make their lives better (new shoes for your cousin, for example, or someone to help your elderly neighbor take out the trash). It doesn't have to be monumental or expensive; just think of anything straightforward that might help these people out. Finally, pick one of them to follow through with and give yourself a finite amount of time to make it happen. For example, "I see the same guy asking for spare change on the corner every morning. At some point this week, I'm going to give him a dollar." It doesn't have to be about money or time, but ideally what you give to the person is something a little beyond what you're accustomed to giving.

I've given quite a bit over the course of my career. I've helped other athletes with advice, money, and other forms of support, but there was one thing in particular I always selfishly guarded for myself: my summers. When I was at the top of my game, I'd spend the whole season in the mountains near Colorado Springs, working my rear end off with drills and a grueling nutrition and intermittent fasting regime. It was a feral time for me—I'd grow out my hair and wouldn't shave so I could spend that much more time focused on the work. I didn't tell anybody what I was doing during the "off-season," and I certainly didn't invite anyone to join me.

But then my friend Ian (the same Ian on my personal board of directors) started asking questions and wanted to know if he could come with me. *Hell no*, I thought. I wasn't about to let anybody mess up my good thing because I was convinced that those summers were one of the things that gave me the edge. While my competitors were off somewhere relaxing with their families and snacking away all summer, I was kicking ass and training way harder than any of them. Even so, something told me to relent, so I invited Ian to join me, and what happened as a result surprised me. Having Ian there with me actually helped me train even harder. Ian pushed me, dove into the training himself, and held me more accountable than I would've been on my own. That taught me a lot about giving, even to people who might be your competitors.

I've thought about this lesson a lot when it comes to the business realm. I honestly believe there's another way than just going about it in a cutthroat, hyper-competitive way. Win-win solutions and partnerships based on mutual benefit are almost always available options, and they're way more adaptive in the end than a dog-eat-dog mentality that just leaves everybody chewed up and bloody. If we do right by each other—especially our teammates and employees—everyone stands to benefit. In that way, giving is central to the paradigm shift I hope we'll see in the business world and the human community at large.

As a final word on giving, I don't want to forget what I urged you to do in chapter 6 about loving yourself. Self-love is critical to the bigger picture, so be sure to regularly give to yourself. What that looks like is up to you—a weekly massage, time alone in the woods, ice cream on your cheat day, a beach vacation to celebrate your new promotion, or a simple self-reminder at just how amazingly awesome you are. Let your generosity include everyone, beginning with yourself.

IT'S EASY TO KEEP ON THE PATH
WHEN THE JOURNEY'S EASY.

GRIT

We've been primed in the United States to look for the easy solution, the product we can order online that will solve all our problems.

We're a culture of miracle cures, seven-day programs promising overnight change, and on-sale quick fixes that offer fast solutions at a discount. Any marketer worth their salt over the past century or more knows that when things get difficult, inconvenient, or uncomfortable, our first response is usually to find the quickest exit door and buy our way out. We're more willing to spend thousands on elective surgery than we are to keep at it in the gym or do the hard work of self-acceptance. If a product pops up on our Facebook feed that says it will help with the struggle, those of us with money have little trouble clicking the link and paying for it. It's as if we're allergic to pain, uncertainty, and the unknown. Even when we know that discipline and change is good for us, most of us choose to revert to what we know, even if it's detrimental, because it offers us familiarity, solid ground, and control.

Grit is the opposite of all of that. Grit is mental stamina, resilience, and toughness for when the path gets strange and difficult. It's making the best with what we have around the house, rather than buying that shiny new product that won't deliver anyway. It's DIY and helping others DIThemselves too. Grit is an element of the human spirit that allows us to dig deep and persevere through short-term pain to eventually reach the destination we're seeking. It's easy to keep on the path when the journey's easy; grit is what keeps us going when it's not.

It's normal to lose sight of why we began in the first place sometimes, especially when we get overwhelmed with discomfort and fear. There's nothing wrong with discouragement or, as I discussed in the last chapter, doubt. But when we let those things run the show and we choose the easy out, we'll never find the grit inside that tells us that more is possible. We all quit things—jobs, relationships, habits (good and bad), and games. Grit is what keeps us from becoming quitters. Grit picks us back up when we fail and steers us toward our purpose-driven goals in life.

Everyone has their own way to get gritty when it matters. I always find it useful to have time-tested techniques to turn to when I need an extra push or assistance, such as a four-step exercise designed by psychologist Gabriele Oettingen, an expert on motivation. Oettingen studied how people felt when they thought about achieving their dreams.[6] One set of study subjects reported feeling joy and contentment when they visualized what their lives would be like after succeeding in a difficult endeavor, and another set of people were instructed to spend time thinking about the obstacles that would stand in the way of achieving their dreams. Guess which group was more successful in meeting their goals in the long run? Yep, the ones who had contemplated the obstacles. It turns out that just dreaming about what you want doesn't make it easier to achieve; you also have to plan for how you'll respond in the face of inevitable challenges. From this research, Oettingen came up with the following framework (WOOP) to help people articulate their goals and strategize ways to achieve them.

PRACTICE
WOOP!

WOOP is an acronym for wish, outcome, obstacles, and plan. Starting with *W*, write out a sentence or two about what you wish you could achieve. It could be anything—a clean kitchen, a Grammy nomination, a new job, a personal best in the 10K. It helps to be as specific as possible, so "to lose weight" isn't nearly as on target as "to lose seven pounds by Christmas." Next, move on to the first *O* and think about the outcomes that achieving that wish might bring you, writing them down as well. Using those previous examples, a clean kitchen might motivate you to cook more and to do so with more happiness and calm; the Grammy would mean accolades and recognition for your musical talent; the new job you're after might be less stressful, more meaningful, and allow you to work from home more; and a better time in the 10K would help you feel healthier, prouder of yourself, and a whole lot faster.

Now comes the fun part. Moving on to the latter two steps of the practice, ponder all the obstacles that stand in your way. For example, perhaps you're too tired to clean the kitchen, everyone else in the house keeps messing it up and adding dirty dishes before you get around to it, or the dishwasher isn't working properly. What is it that stands in your way? List all the problems you can think of and then move on to the final step: the plan.

Break the obstacles down one by one and list the steps to manage them. Continuing on with the messy kitchen example, let's just look at the first obstacle: tiredness. Your plan to deal with that might include taking a walk around the block or making a cup of coffee to perk you up, setting an earlier bedtime to give you more rest during the night, or simply breaking the task down into manageable chunks (cleaning out the oven, for example, or wiping down the counters) you can do here and there throughout the day.

I can't talk about grit without mentioning Angela Duckworth, the premier scholar on the subject, who defines *grit* as intense passion *plus* intense perseverance.[7] Duckworth developed a formula for grit that goes something like this: First, you apply effort to your talent to develop necessary skills; then, you apply effort to your skills to achieve your desired goal. You'll notice that this equation prioritizes effort. In her book, *Grit: The Power of Passion and Perseverance*, Duckworth looks into the life of actor Will Smith, who is known for his intensity and dedication to his craft. "I've never really viewed myself as particularly talented," Smith says. "Where I excel is ridiculous, sickening work ethic . . . I will not be outworked, period. You might have more talent than me, you might be smarter than me, you might be sexier than me. You might be all of those things. You got it on me in nine categories. But if we get on the treadmill together, there's two things: you're getting off first, or I'm going to die. It's really that simple."

Although I don't recommend putting yourself in that sort of peril to achieve your goals, Smith drives home the fact that grit requires serious commitment. My dad tells an amazing, grit-illustrating story similar to this—something he did about twenty-five years ago to save his business.

My father was managing two barber salons at the time, and the second shop became too much for him to be successful with. A renter lined up to take over the space, and my dad had to get all his stuff out of the shop a lot sooner than expected—in fact, he only had a day to do it. But because he didn't have the funds to hire any help, my father worked by himself for fourteen hours straight throughout the night to move every single piece of equipment out. To keep himself motivated, he kept Tchaikovsky on full blast the whole time. Later on, when one of those symphonies came on the radio, my dad told me the story. "I get so much energy listening to this music," he said. "I was like a crazed madman that night. I didn't know where the next dollar was going to come from, but I knew that I needed to save every penny I had, and all that equipment was worth money. You were at home sleeping, and there I was, hammering away in this office park, ripping things from the wall, and getting every single thing I could out of there."

That's the kind of purpose, love, resourcefulness, and grit my dad exemplifies. He wasn't going to let anything go to waste in that situation, and he worked harder and longer than almost anyone else would have in that situation to make sure that we were going to be okay. Sometimes that's what it takes, and you have to summon up a warrior-like mentality to meet the challenges in front of you. When you're under duress, pain, chaos, and uncertainty, that's when grit matters most.

As a final note, consistency is paramount when it comes to grit. As Caroline Adams Miller notes, "If you demonstrate self-control one day, but not regularly, or you can persist when you want to, but not most of the time, then you will not cultivate authentic grit—instead, you are someone who is dabbling in grit."[8] Just as with gratitude, teamwork, self-confidence, curiosity, love, purpose, and so much else, it takes attentive practice to foster grit. So I invite you to find the exercises that work for you in this book, incorporate them into your life, and become more than a dabbler in life. That's what it's going to take for you to move forward through the challenges to come and fulfill your purpose.

GEARING UP

Gearing up is somewhat like the final stage of the WOOP practice you did a couple of pages back. Gearing up is about taking bold action toward the goals you've set for yourself and prepping yourself mentally and physically for the challenges ahead. Often that means leveling up with a growth-oriented mindset, new skills, or innovative techniques to help you succeed.

When I think back to my early days as a public speaker, I actually cringe. Watching those old videos and listening to my clumsy attempts to connect with an audience is just painful. I had no idea what I was doing, and what's worse is that I didn't recognize what a terrible job I was doing. Thankfully, at some point I received some useful feedback, and I decided to put some work into it, mainly by paying attention to the way I communicated throughout the day. Every interaction became an opportunity to be more mindful of my tone, cadence, variation of expression, and thoughtful pausing. I used every conversation as a practice round—with friends, family, and colleagues. Paying attention to my speech regularly like that is one of the things that helped me level up.

GEARING UP ALSO MEANS FOCUSING ON THE BASICS—IDENTIFYING THE FUNDAMENTAL REQUIREMENTS FOR MEETING YOUR GOALS AND PUTTING THE WORK IN.

Gearing up also involves learning to think of yourself (and present yourself) in new ways. The goals you're after in life should be in alignment with your developing identity, even if that identity is new to you and feels like unfamiliar territory. For me to become a confident and more-than-just-competent public speaker, I had to learn new skills, practice them a lot, and put myself in front of audiences, but I also had to start thinking of myself as a confident presenter. In the same way, a person whose hard pivot involves moving from managing sales in someone else's company to starting up their own business and becoming a CEO will at some point require them to assume the identity of a CEO, and very likely earlier than they're ready for it. Reinvention also means retraining the thoughts that grounded your former identity. It also means changing the expectations you have for yourself. How would a CEO act in this situation? How would they respond to this report? What kind of CEO do I want to be when it comes to consulting with my team? Asking yourself questions like these are part of how you'll grow into the new version of yourself.

On a practical note, gearing up also means focusing on the basics—identifying the fundamental requirements for meeting your goals and putting the work in. I always start by identifying the low-hanging fruit. What helps me feel my best? What solutions are immediately at hand? What are the obvious first steps? What choices will make the most impact moving forward? Answering these questions for myself helps me gain momentum and confidence so I can climb higher and grab some of the less accessible and tastier fruit higher up in the proverbial tree. Maybe it's my training as an athlete, but for me the lowest hanging fruit usually has something to do with how I'm eating, moving, or sleeping.

These might sound simplistic to you, but I've always found these three to be the basic building blocks of optimal performance. There's no way I'm gearing up unless I have them dialed in because letting any of them slide will always result in unnecessary obstacles, and usually the kind of obstacles that have wide-reaching effects—feeling overwhelmed and distracted, for example, or experiencing low energy and the inability to focus.

If I discover I'm not eating well, I change my diet, cut out the junk food, or prep healthy meals in the morning and commit to just eating that food for the rest of the day. Those solutions are almost always at hand to make my body feel stronger and better fueled. It's the same thing with movement—like most people, I need regular exercise to thrive, but sometimes it's a challenge to plan the day around physical activities. That being said, it's not hard to take a break to stretch, walk around the block, or call a friend for extra motivation to go to the gym. And sleep means everything when it comes to mental clarity and alertness. I break good sleep down into three categories: duration, consistency, and quality. If any of these three are off, chances are I'm off too. But, again, solutions to these aren't hard to come by. For example, it's not that hard to make the decision to hop in bed thirty minutes early as opposed to checking out something new on Netflix or even committing to doing so for three or four days until you feel more rested. So, if you're having trouble identifying your own low-hanging fruit when it comes to gearing up, I recommend starting with eating, moving, and sleeping. Getting those three on point will help you with everything else.

When it comes to gearing up, I always think about Tommy Caldwell, who's widely considered the greatest all-around rock climber on the planet. In addition to surviving being taken hostage in Kyrgyzstan, Caldwell accidentally lost much of his left index finger in a carpentry accident.

As you might guess, fingers are sort of important in rock climbing. Climbers, more than most athletes in other sports, require the dexterity and strength of all ten fingers to successfully ascend whatever wall or mountain they're climbing. Sometimes the holds they need to grab are just tiny slivers of protruding granite, less than a quarter of an inch wide. It's hard for a fly to rest on something that small, let alone a grown man who needs to suspend his entire body weight from it. Because of this, everyone told Caldwell that his climbing career was over. Without that crucial finger, he'd never be able to grasp the holds sufficiently (not to mention safely).

Instead of quitting, Caldwell geared up. He actually had about half of his finger left, so he decided to put that knuckle through the most intense training you can imagine. He lifted more weight with it than most gym buffs can bench press, and he spent a year teaching that half finger to grip and bend in such a way that Caldwell could resume climbing. After seven years of plotting his route, practicing new maneuvers, and months of prepping on the lower sections of the climb, Caldwell tackled one of the most difficult climbs in the world: the Dawn Wall of El Capitan in Yosemite.[9] Talk about stretching for a goal that's supposedly out of reach! Caldwell's pivot is the very stuff of gearing up to fulfill your purpose.

PRACTICE
THE BIG PREP

Think about some of the suggestions I mentioned in this section. What speaks to you? Whether it's learning or honing a new skill to help you succeed, assuming the thoughts and behaviors of your new identity, or just getting a better night's sleep to help you remain focused for the challenging day you have ahead, list two or three ways you can gear up. What are your low-hanging fruit? What actions will help you get a running start? Once you've identified a handful of clear action items, choose one of them and commit to doing it as soon as possible. And whatever you choose, be sure to remind yourself why you're doing it and exactly how this particular form of gearing up is going to benefit you.

GO

There's not much I want to say about this Golden Principle. In fact, the less said at this point, the better. When it's time to go, it's time to go.

When I'm at the go point in life, it signifies so much that's come before: I've practiced gratitude and self-love, I've devoted my time and resources to the cause and to others, I've applied grit through various challenges, and I've geared up to face whatever's coming next. The only thing left to do is to do it.

Start the race. Do your best. Try it out in the world. It doesn't have to work perfectly on your first try. In fact, it probably won't. Keep going, keep learning, and remember that the outcome isn't up to you. Only your preparation and effort are up to you. But not much happens without that.

I'm a big dreamer. I always have been. I love setting audacious goals and gearing up for them, but sometimes it's hard for me to get going. I can get caught up hanging out too long in the analysis phase, trying to forecast all the possible outcomes of my actions, and predicting all sorts of things that are way beyond my control. It's easy to get stuck there. At some point, though, you have to acknowledge that it's time to go. It's unlikely that you'll ever feel 100 percent ready to face the challenges in front of you, and that's okay. Nobody does.

"The mature human being goes about doing what needs to be done regardless of whether that person feels great or terrible," David Reynolds writes in *Constructive Living*.[10] The book is an excellent guide for accepting our emotional process while still driving ourselves to take consistent action. Reynolds makes the point that while our feelings and behaviors are intimately linked, there is a significant difference between the two. We generally can't control how we feel, but we definitely can control how we behave, so when you commit to taking disciplined action, you have no choice but to tackle what you've set out to do, even on the days when you're not feeling optimal. Because in the context of reaching our goals, our ever-shifting feelings should not govern our commitment to showing up and doing what we've prepped so long to do.

PRACTICE
JUST GO

Whatever *go* looks like for you, just do it. The time for practices and exercises is over. Briefly reflect on all your preparation so far—all your hard work and the hard decisions you've had to make in service of your hard pivot—and then make the leap. Just do it. Just go.

PIVOT POINTS

- Gratitude steers your mind away from habitual negativity.
- Gratitude is the opposite of entitlement.
- Giving to others is one of our basic human needs.
- When you do right by others, everyone benefits.
- Grit is what gets us through discomfort, inconvenience, hardship, and failure.
- We all have grit, but it isn't a given. It takes commitment and consistent effort over time.
- Gearing up means prepping yourself for the challenges ahead.
- Diligently taking care of the basics (for example, adequate sleep, diet, and exercise) is an essential way to gear up.
- At some point, you just have to go. Make a start, try it out, and do your best.
- Go rarely means winning right out of the gate.

CHAPTER NINE

Bringing It All Home

Make your lives a masterpiece, you only get one canvas.[1]

E. A. BUCCHIANERI

At every Olympics there is an opening ceremony that's watched around the world. Right before the ceremony, all the competitors are together in one holding room next to the main arena. You walk into that room with your uniform on and with all your teammates flanking you. There's an indescribable buzz in the air. Everyone there is a champion. Everyone in that room is among the top athletes in their chosen sport. Everyone there has spent a good portion of their life training for the events that will unfold over the next few weeks. The athletes mingle, shake hands, congratulate each other, take pictures, and so on. From each of the Games I've attended (2002, 2006, and 2010), this is the moment I remember that most embodies the spirit of the Games. The whole experience is one of incredible potential and radiant excellence. Then we get the cue to enter the arena, and all that built-up energy gets transmitted around the globe.

That's where you are right now. You've worked so hard to get to this moment, and now's your time to step into the light.

As I've mentioned several times in the book, hard pivots aren't easy. And when it comes to reinventing yourself, losing a long-held identity can be frightening, even terrifying to some. My own Great Divorce from who I was as an Olympian shook me to my core, but even in my darkest moments, I knew I had to push through whatever came next because I simply couldn't stay where I was. Maybe I had another Games in me, maybe I didn't, but I had no doubt that the end was coming, that it was time for me to move on.

So that's what I did. I put my medals away and embarked on a long, circuitous journey to clarify my purpose, make a new career for myself, and develop a new identity, one that went way beyond who Apolo the Olympian had been. Thankfully, I didn't have to leave everything behind. All the core attributes that made me an exceptional athlete—speed, dedication, and curiosity—came in handy for the challenges to come. Over time, I realized that my purpose had a lot to do with inspiring people to be their best, and my commitment to a growth mindset (along with my newfound skills of self-love and empathy) helped me persevere through the inevitable obstacles and setbacks. And, of course, I never could have done it alone. Without the help of Bianca and my personal board of directors, I'd still be back there on the path somewhere, trying to figure it all out by myself (and failing).

The point is that I did it. I'm still doing it, really. And because I'm doing it and know what it takes, I know you can do it too.

> PART OF YOU IS GOING TO SAY NO. IT'LL TELL YOU TO STOP, TO GO BACK, TO BELIEVE THAT YOU WERE NUTS FOR EVER THINKING YOU COULD REINVENT YOURSELF.

Hard Pivot is about showing you what I know works. All the insights and practices in this book are what I used to get where I am, and I still use them to this day, so I'm living proof that they work. I don't expect everything to click for you. Some exercises will speak to you more than others, and some sections will fire you up, whereas others will fall flat. That's to be expected, and I invite you to try everything out, make your own adjustments, come up with your own techniques that facilitate your hard pivot, and find your unique way to persevere and align yourself with your highest goals.

Whatever has occurred in your life up until now—no matter your triumphs, struggles, and mistakes—you already possess a lot of the tools you'll need to navigate what's coming next. And with gratitude, giving, grit, and gearing up, you'll find yourself at go. Do what you can to get ready, but remember that *ready* is a state of mind, and you'll never know what you're capable of until you actually go.

Part of you is going to say *no*. It'll tell you to stop, to go back, to believe that you were nuts for ever thinking you could reinvent yourself. That's to be expected too. It's not your ego's job to strike out on new adventures; your ego's job is to protect you, to provide you with the bare necessities, to keep you safe, to remind you of your limits. When faced with challenges, your ego is primed to make you cautious, which is why it tells you that the best course of action is to turn back, seek shelter, and stick with what you know. So if your ego hasn't already been chattering in your ear in this way, go ahead and expect it. Thank it for trying to help you and then move on.

You can trust yourself. Instead of going back, you can lean into the curve, pick up momentum, and speed down the back side of the track to success. In that pivotal moment, you might even find that you're having the most fun you've ever had in your life. You're in flow. You're playing. You're enjoying your precious life. And you're winning.

THE PURE PLEASURE OF SETTING YOUR GOALS AND WORKING TO MEET THEM

There is nothing more satisfying than setting a goal just beyond the reach of what you think you can achieve and then systematically going for it, day after day after day. Dedicating yourself fully to something or someone unlocks an energy you might not have had before—in fact, it might feel unfamiliar to you, even strange. Even so, I think most of us know that we perform our best when we're totally committed and immersed in the process, when we see our full potential and set an intention to reach it. We begin to embody the very thing that we want to change in ourselves. In a way, it's magic. And it's utterly exciting. That excitement fuels our enthusiasm, which feeds our drive and commitment even more.

Other than skating, I haven't consistently applied myself to other sports, but that's not to say that I haven't competed here and there in other events. A lot of people know that I won *Dancing with the Stars*, but I also decided to compete in the Ironman® Triathlon in 2014 after being challenged by my good friend and top triathlete, Mark Fretta. For the longest time, I didn't really get triathlons. They're mostly full of non-professional athletes who pour their guts into a soul-crushingly difficult event that doesn't seem to amount to a lot from the outside. Even so, I was up for Mark's challenge. As someone who spent much of his life competing in an event that was done in under a minute, I thought trying the opposite would be a nice twist.

The Ironman is a 2.4-mile swim, a 112-mile bike ride, and a 26.2-mile (full marathon length) run to end it. I asked Mark how long he thought it might take me to complete the race.

"Well," he said. "It would be sort of amazing if you could do it in under eleven hours."

"How about in under ten?" I teased him.

"No way," he replied. "You can just forget about that. You'll never do it in under ten hours."

Well, he said that to the wrong guy. I finished in nine hours and fifty-two minutes, and I trained like mad to do it. The whole process was utterly exhausting and enjoyable, but what I most took away from that experience happened during the last six miles of the run.

That's when I got it. The Ironman isn't just about how fast you can do it; it's about what it takes to complete the race. You don't actually know if you're going to finish until that final stretch, and well before then, you've already pushed yourself beyond your known physical limits. The thrill isn't in winning; it's in sticking to it the whole time. Even when the Ironman feels impossibly painful and painfully impossible to complete, you just keep going, simply to prove to yourself that, no matter what, you're going to cross that finish line. Your satisfaction comes from the very doing of the thing you set out to do.

I'm a physical guy, so I regularly encourage people to set physical fitness goals for themselves and put the work in to meet them. The Ironman Triathlon isn't for everyone (truthfully, it's not for most people), but most of us can find some means of feeling active and potent in our bodies. That certainly doesn't have to take the form of something drastic like the Ironman or the Boston Marathon or swimming across an expanse of open water, but there are countless other reachable ways to set fitness goals for yourself. Your body is a wonderful playground for developing grit and showing up every day, even when you don't feel like it.

Of course, it's not important that your goals have a physical component. Lots of people aren't able-bodied enough to take on those sorts of challenges, and that's utterly okay. The point is to set goals for yourself and put in the work to meet them. There're thousands of ways to cultivate grit without hitting the gym. Grit isn't about running or swimming or riding a bike or any of that; it's about setting hard and meaningful goals and putting in the work to achieve them. And if you commit yourself and persevere through hardship, that's grit. Accomplishing those goals is just extra.

If you set out to do hard things, you'll come to see yourself as someone who isn't fixed in your abilities or boxed in by whatever set of limitations or struggles you personally have to deal with. You'll discover that you aren't stuck. You can do something different. You can change.

KEEPING TRACK

As the partner at a venture capital firm, I work daily with top-tier data-science and engineering-based decision-makers to figure out which companies to invest in. Even though we're implementing the latest AI and algorithmic tools, I also operate on my gut instincts. I've always been that way. My particular background matches well with my partners' mathematical rigor, but that doesn't mean that I can just sit back, do my thing, and leave all the brainwork up to them. Even though they're the experts, I still have to learn more about financial instruments, for example, and that often leaves me feeling overwhelmed, especially whenever we kick off a new project. Day one is excruciating for me. Day three is still grueling. Thirty days in, things are still hard, but there's been a substantial change. By day sixty, I'm kind of getting it, and a couple of months later, I hit my groove. That doesn't mean that it isn't hard anymore; it just means that I've worked out the major kinks, I've kept going, and I'm handling it. And to think that I felt like quitting in that first week.

I've talked about the power of journaling in chapter 3 and elsewhere. Journaling is how I keep track of my goals, aspirations, and progress. It's how I know that no matter how impossible the first day feels, it always gets better. For this reason alone, I recommend journaling to record the steps along your path to reinvention. Remind yourself how it's going and what's important. Write it all down and hold yourself accountable.

You ARE THE SUM OF YOUR EXPERIENCES—YOUR WINS AND LOSSES AND EVERYTHING IN BETWEEN.

If journaling just isn't for you, ask one of your starting five or another trusted friend to help. Have them monitor your progress, especially when it comes to gearing up to meet the expectations you've set for yourself. Have them also remind you of your failures, doubts, and missteps. These are just as valuable to note and learn from as the wins that are worth writing down.

Keeping track is different from highlighting the shiny bits in life. Holding yourself accountable means going beyond what you might show the world on LinkedIn or Facebook. Your accomplishments and best selfies don't tell the whole story; most of the time, they don't even tell the more interesting parts of your story. For the sake of your own growth, recognize your triumphs, but don't turn away from the times you fell on your face. Not to dwell on them and yank yourself down, but to learn and grow. You are the sum of your experiences—your wins and losses and everything in between. When you're able to see all of it clearly and accept yourself no matter what, moving forward through the challenges ahead is a cinch.

THE IMPORTANCE OF RESETTING

I've had to reset my life several times, including some I've already talked about in this book. Sometimes resetting means a pivot in your life, and sometimes it just means getting right with what you set out to do.

I still had braces when I won the US speed-skating trials. I was just fourteen, and I was favored to win a spot on the Olympic team the next year. It was supposed to be everything I ever wanted, and it was even more meaningful on another level because those Olympics were going to be held in Nagano, Japan, where my dad's side of the family lives. The opportunity for my father to bring his son back home and have all our relatives watch would have been so redemptive for us. They never approved of him leaving Japan to start a new life in America, and me competing in the Olympics there would have shown them that it wasn't all for nothing.

Except it didn't happen. And it didn't happen because when it came time to go (make the team), I hadn't geared up properly. I was just a kid at the time, so it was understandable, but I basically phoned it in and didn't train as I should have. So when the trials came around, I bombed. Utterly. I came in dead last. Within one year, I'd gone from being the most-talked-about athlete in speed skating to being written off as just another kid who couldn't hack it.

But my dad knew otherwise. He believed in me, but he also knew I'd just gone through the motions and hadn't put in the work. No matter what came next for me—whether I kept with speed skating or did something else—my dad wanted me to know the power of dedication, as well as the consequences of slacking off. So he took me to a remote retreat center outside of Seattle and left me there. This was one of his tough love moments I mentioned in chapter 6.

I had a cabin to stay in, but not much else. It seemed like a witness protection center, to be honest. I didn't see anyone, I didn't have TV, and I could only make calls on a pay phone. This was way before all the distractions we're so accustomed to these days, so it was the perfect situation to just be with myself and figure out my life direction in all that solitude. In a simplified environment like that, there's space to find yourself if you try. I spent hours running in the rain and walking around in nature while it was dark, cloudy, and beautiful in all the ways the Pacific Northwest can be. The moody environment reflected the insecurities and fears I was wrestling with inside. I felt like I'd been a disappointment to my father and a failure to the speed-skating community, and I filled my journal with questions and explorations and random ramblings. Why did I throw away such an opportunity? Why was I feeling the way I did about it? I wrote everything out, and gradually the answers came to me.

I knew I hadn't touched my potential yet. I'd slacked off, and I hadn't made the team because of it, and all the feelings I had as a consequence came as the result of my own actions. I knew that I couldn't live with myself unless I tried again and gave it everything I had, regardless of the outcome. I needed my dad and my teammates to see the real me.

Even though it would be years until I started practicing the Five Golden Principles, the seeds of their power were already planted in me. And so I got gritty and wrote down exactly how I was going to change the way I ate, slept, and trained. I vowed to throw out anything in my life that wasn't conducive to making me a better athlete. I told myself I wouldn't quit when it got tough. And just like that, I was resolved. I called my dad and told him everything I'd discovered, as well as everything I'd resolved.

That experience taught me the value of resetting. I've had to revisit that place of solitude in nature several times since then. I've had to remove myself in order to quiet my mind, truly slow down, and listen to my heart. That's what it takes sometimes to find out what's important and nonnegotiable for me, away from the influence of what other people and the world wants from me.

I know that most people can't just get up and go on retreat for a couple of weeks whenever the mood strikes them. You don't have to do that. Resetting just means finding some way to separate yourself from your regular routine, whether it means going for a long walk alone in the woods, grabbing thirty minutes to reflect with your notebook, or turning off all the devices and sitting by yourself in your room for a couple of hours. Whatever works for you, resetting is worth it. And you'll find that the benefits that come from doing so after you "come back" are exponential. You'll return to your life clarified, with new insights and ideas for improvement that you never would have come up with otherwise.

THAT'S ONE PIVOT FOR YOU, ONE GIANT PIVOT FOR HUMANKIND

I know I'm not alone in thinking that the whole world today needs a hard pivot. In the aftermath of the global pandemic and the ongoing urgency of income disparity and climate disruption (not to mention the ongoing disruption of the political climate), the issue of a larger transformation for the benefit of all is more pressing than ever. I'll take a shot here and say that one of our issues is giving—or, rather, the opposite of giving. We can no longer thrive with the mentality that only the strongest will survive, that we have to kill or be killed, and that it's us against them, always. We can't keep living like that as a species and expect to survive.

Fortunately, the great truth is that we have it in us to be way more cooperative than we are destructive. Otherwise, we never would have made it this far in our evolution as a species. So if we want the world to be safer, more sustainable, more prosperous, more joy-filled, and a place where people can truly thrive, we need to access our capacity for empathy, vulnerability, and understanding. Because generosity is nothing without that.

I'm all for competing, but when the stakes are so high, we need the world to take a hard pivot away from a competition-first mindset and instead choose to collaborate so we can actually commit to defeating the disastrous effects of inequality, pollution, racism, fanaticism, the destruction of the environment, and so on. We need a hard pivot. We need the velocity of decision-making to be aggressive and immediate on a global scale. But how can we get the planet to turn on a dime and speed the other way?

Clearly, I don't have all the answers. No one person does, which is sort of the point. We have to work together—for each other and for ourselves.

JUST BECAUSE YOU WEREN'T SUCCESSFUL THIS TIME DOESN'T MEAN YOU WON'T BE SUCCESSFUL THE NEXT TIME YOU TRY.

Here's one place to start: when it feels like the world is falling down all around you and you begin to feel hopeless and lost, find what's working and give thanks for it. There's always something to feel grateful for—always. Just find that thing and go from there. Find others to work with, find others who will support you and help you thrive, and find those, too, who need your gifts. And keep going, understanding that the trials are just a part of it. No matter the expectations, keep at it, and remind yourself of the undeniable power of your grit. Then gear up and go. Just do it. The world is calling you to do it.

When you're on the rink, you can feel the air on your face as you head around the first turn. You're crouched in an aerodynamic position as you cross your left foot over the heel of your right, and you focus on keeping your nose, knees, and toes in alignment. You feel the tension building, that g-force pull on your hips and core, making you feel taut and relaxed into the suspension at the same time. That's when you catapult yourself like a slingshot around the next turn, faster and faster . . .

Maybe you cross the line first and beat your best time. Maybe you fall or crash into the wall and it hurts. Sometimes a lot. But know that life *requires* this hard pivot of you, and just because you weren't successful this time doesn't mean you won't be successful the next time you try. So reset and start again. Get back up to speed, to that incredible corner velocity, even if you have to try it over and over again. Sometimes, you have to go when you're not fully ready, and that's okay too. Gear up, build speed, and hit the next pivot like you've never done before.

Wherever you are in your pivot—whatever strange land your journey of reinvention has brought you to—you can always take the next step forward. Before you know it, you're someplace else, and you're looking back with the benefits and hard-won lessons of hindsight. First you crawl, then you walk, and then you sprint (or, for some of us, skate). Progressing like that takes consistent effort, belief, and time.

No doubt that we all have our struggles, and some of us are hindered by hardship and trauma. No doubt there are tremendous challenges facing our species. Even so, it's almost always within our power to change our behaviors, learn from where we've been, and get back at it. As fast as we seem to be going in one direction, we can always reach down with one confident hand and glide the other way with a few clear, determined strides. That hard pivot is always within reach.

PIVOT POINTS

- Try out the practices in this book, find out what works best for you, and make any necessary adjustments.
- On the journey to reinvention, part of you will always tell yourself to turn back. Your ego always wants you to stay with what's known and what's safe.
- Physical activity and exercise of any sort is a reliable way to show up regularly and develop grit.
- Find ways (like journaling) to keep track of your progress.
- Working together is good for all of us. It's also necessary if we want to change the world for the better.

Acknowledgments

Thank you . . .

To my father: For your philosophical teaching and everlasting support and love. For reminding me to constantly question my true north, listen to my heart and soul, and remain committed to what is possible.

To Bianca: You've shown so much patience, thoughtfulness, and the power of simplicity in a world filled with distractions. You are my love.

To Ian: You are family to me. Your work, kindness, selflessness, friendship, support, and unwavering honesty hold me up when I am shaky!

To John Schaeffer: You've shown me how deep the reservoir of potential can be. You've helped me take "I can't" into "I can," or at the very least, I will!

To the Sounds True team: I couldn't have been partnered with a better team. You have shown patience, creativity, and support and have gone above and beyond expectations.

To Maria: Every lesson, question, and thought has impacted the perceptions of my reality. Thank you for pushing me to seek the truth, do what I feel is right, and always give my all.

And to YOU, the reader: The journey is never easy; it is volatile and often frightening. Thank you for trusting in these pages but, more importantly, for showing yourself what can go right vs. what might go wrong. The hard pivot is a necessity. And you are halfway around that corner. Trust in your process, and show up fully.

Notes

INTRODUCTION What Now?

1. Stephen Mitchell, *Tao Te Ching* (New York: Harper & Row, 1988).
2. Douglas Malloch, *In Forest Land* (Chicago: American Lumberman, 1910).

CHAPTER ONE The Great Divorce

1. Viktor Frankl, *Man's Search for Meaning* (Boston: Beacon Press, 2006).
2. Diamond Dallas Page, *Positively Unstoppable: The Art of Owning It* (New York: Rodale, 2019), 114.
3. Joseph Campbell, *The Hero's Journey* (Novato, CA: New World Library, 1990).

CHAPTER TWO Your Starting Five

1. Joseph Lash, *Helen and Teacher* (Cambridge, UK: Perseus, 1980).
2. Connie Stemmle, "You Are the Average of the Five People Quote: 5 Lessons," Develop Good Habits, February 9, 2021, developgoodhabits.com/five-people/.

CHAPTER THREE Cultivating Belief

1. Pema Chödrön, *When Things Fall Apart* (Boulder, CO: Shambhala, 2016).
2. Phillippa Lally et al., "How Are Habits Formed: Modelling Habit Formation in the Real World," *European Journal of Social Psychology* 40, no. 6 (October 2010): 998–1009, onlinelibrary.wiley.com/doi/abs/10.1002/ejsp.674.
3. Widely attributed to Rumi, but no precise source found. goodreads.com /quotes/7368103-wear-gratitude-like-a -cloak-and-it-will-feed-every.

4. Intelligent Change, *The Five-Minute Journal,*
   intelligentchange.com/products/the-five-minute-journal.

5. Brad Stulberg and Steve Magness, *Peak Performance:
   Elevate Your Game, Avoid Burnout, and Thrive with the
   New Science of Success* (New York: Rodale, 2017).

6. Confucius, *The Analects,* trans. D. C. Lau
   (London, UK: Penguin Books, 1979).

7. Quote Investigator, "I Have Gotten a Lot of Results!
   I Know Several Thousand Things That Won't Work,"
   quoteinvestigator.com/2012/07/31/edison-lot-results/.

CHAPTER FOUR **The Work Is the Shortcut**

1. Lucius Annaeus Seneca, *Seneca Stoicism Collection,*
   trans. Aubrey Stewart and Richard Gummere,
   independently published, 2021.

2. Meb Keflezighi, *Meb for Mortals* (New York: Rodale, 2015).

3. Doug Farr, "10 Years Later, Herm Edwards' 'You PLAY to WIN
   the GAME!!' Rant Still Resonates," October 26, 2012,
   sports.yahoo.com/blogs/shutdown-corner/10-years-later
   -herm-edwards-play-win-game-225650424—nfl.html.

CHAPTER FIVE **Relentless Curiosity**

1. Albert Einstein, *The Ultimate Quotable Einstein*
   (Princeton, NJ: Princeton University Press, 2010).

2. "'There's No Losing, Only Learning. There's No
   Failure, Only Opportunities . . .' -Pitbull," August 10,
   2018, youtube.com/watch?v=sqi8MN9GGCs.

3. Áine Cain, "Inside the Daily Routine of 87-Year-Old
   Warren Buffett, Who Loves McDonald's, Spends 80% of His
   Workday Reading, and Unwinds by Playing the Ukulele,"
   September 1, 2017, Business Insider, businessinsider.com
   /warren-buffett-daily-routine-2017-8.

4. Erika Andersen, "10 Quotes from the 'First Lady of
   the World,'" *Forbes*, January 10, 2013, forbes.com
   /sites/erikaandersen/2013/01/10/10-quotes-from
   -the-first-lady-of-the-world/?sh=5131cd14272b/.

CHAPTER SIX **Choose Love**

1. Leo Buscaglia, *Love: What Life Is All About*
   (New York: Fawcett Columbine, 1972).
2. Buscaglia, *Love.*
3. Rick Hanson, *Hardwiring Happiness*
   (New York: Harmony Books, 2013).
4. Erich Fromm, *The Art of Loving* (New York: Harper & Row, 1956).

CHAPTER SEVEN **Finding Your Purpose**

1. Martin Luther King Jr., *Strength to Love*
   (Minneapolis: Fortress Press, 2010).
2. Viktor Frankl, *Man's Search for Meaning* (Boston: Beacon Press, 2006).
3. Andrew Steptoe and Daisy Fancourt, "Leading a Meaningful
   Life at Older Ages and Its Relationship with Social Engagement,
   Prosperity, Health, Biology, and Time Use," *PNAS* 116, no. 4
   (January 2019): 1207–1212, pnas.org/content/116/4/1207.
4. The Jane Goodall Institute UK, "Biography,"
   janegoodall.org.uk/jane-goodall/biography.
5. Dena M. Bravata et al., "Commentary: Prevalence, Predictors,
   and Treatment of Imposter Syndrome: A Systemic Review,"
   Journal of Mental Health and Clinical Psychology, August 24, 2020,
   mentalhealthjournal.org/articles/commentary-prevalence-predictors
   -and-treatment-of-imposter-syndrome-a-systematic-review.html.

CHAPTER EIGHT **The Five Golden Principles**

1. Peter Grier, "JFK Assassination: President Kennedy's Last
   Veterans Day," *Christian Science Monitor*, November 11, 2013,
   csmonitor.com/USA/Politics/Decoder/2013/1111/JFK
   -assassination-President-Kennedy-s-last-Veterans-Day.
2. R. A. Emmons and M. E. McCullough, "Counting Blessings
   Versus Burdens: An Experimental Investigation of
   Gratitude and Subjective Well-Being in Daily Life," *Journal
   of Personality and Social Psychology* 84, no. 2 (February
   2003): 377–89, pubmed.ncbi.nlm.nih.gov/12585811/.
3. Amy Morin, "7 Scientifically Proven Benefits of Gratitude
   That Will Motivate You to Give Thanks Year-Round," *Forbes,*

November 23, 2014, forbes.com/sites/amymorin/2014/11
/23/7-scientifically-proven-benefits-of-gratitude-that-will
-motivate-you-to-give-thanks-year-round/?sh=7e096397183c.

4. Jason Marsh, "Tips for Keeping a Gratitude Journal,"
Greater Good, November 17, 2011, greatergood.berkeley.edu
/article/item/tips_for_keeping_a_gratitude_journal.

5. Adam Grant, *Give and Take* (New York: Viking, 2013).

6. Gabriele Oettingen and Klaus Michael Reininger,
"The Power of Prospection: Mental Contrasting and Behavior
Change," *Social and Personality Psychology Compass* 10, no. 11
(November 2016): 591–604, doi.org/10.1111/spc3.12271.

7. Angela Duckworth, *Grit: The Power of Passion and
Perseverance* (New York: Scribner, 2016).

8. Caroline Adams Miller, *Getting Grit: The Evidence-
Based Approach to Cultivating Passion, Perseverance,
and Purpose* (Boulder, CO: Sounds True, 2017).

9. Tommy Caldwell, *The Push* (New York: Penguin, 2017).

10. David Reynolds, *Constructive Living* (Honolulu:
University of Hawaii Press, 1984).

CHAPTER NINE **Bringing It All Home**

1. E. A. Bucchianeri, *Brushstrokes of a Gadfly*
(New York: Batalha, 2018).

About the Author

Apolo Anton Ohno claimed his first major speed skating title at the US Championships at the age of fourteen—after just six months of training. Over the next decade and a half, he went from kid prodigy to the most decorated US Winter Olympian in history—a title he still holds—earning eight Olympic medals in short track speed skating across the 2002, 2006, and 2010 Winter Games.

Following the Vancouver 2010 Olympic Games, Apolo took his understanding of sport psychology and his personal experience with success and setbacks to develop a resilient and mission-driven approach to life. His 2011 book *Zero Regrets* became a *New York Times* bestseller.

Apolo remains involved in the Olympic movement. He was an NBC sports analyst for the Sochi 2014 and Pyeongchang 2018 Winter Games and is a global ambassador for the Special Olympics and the Winter Olympics. He is currently on the bid committees for the Winter Games in Salt Lake City, Utah, and the 2028 Summer Games in Los Angeles, California. He has also continued to push himself in the world of sport, winning season four of ABC's hit reality show *Dancing with the Stars* and finishing the 2014 Ironman World Championship Triathlon in Kona, Hawaii in less than ten hours.

Apolo has spent much of the past decade traveling the world and translating his successes and life lessons to business. The bulk of this time in Asia was spent immersed in exploration of various business sectors ranging from rare earth mining and development to infrastructure and software. He also completed the executive education curriculum at the Wharton School of the University of Pennsylvania, alongside executive-track businesspeople from some of the world's top companies. Through his speaking engagements with hundreds of organizations—from Fortune 100 companies to nonprofits—Apolo has helped business leaders think about what it takes to develop a high-performance mindset and remain relevant in a world in which uncertainty is the norm, focusing on how individuals—be they executives or front-line employees—find motivation and consistently do their best work. He is passionate about helping others not only achieve but exceed what they believe to be possible in both life and business.

Apolo's most recent work has centered on the concept of reinvention—an undertaking in which he has demonstrated mastery. His life has been defined not just by performing at the highest possible level in various arenas but also by regularly pursuing new goals and tackling new challenges, all while maintaining his iconic positive attitude and unmatched energy. Apolo continues to bring these attributes to every new endeavor and every business engagement. To learn more, find Apolo on Instagram, Twitter, Facebook, and at apoloohno.com.

About Sounds True

Sounds True is a multimedia publisher whose mission is to inspire and support personal transformation and spiritual awakening. Founded in 1985 and located in Boulder, Colorado, we work with many of the leading spiritual teachers, thinkers, healers, and visionary artists of our time. We strive with every title to preserve the essential "living wisdom" of the author or artist. It is our goal to create products that not only provide information to a reader or listener but also embody the quality of a wisdom transmission.

For those seeking genuine transformation, Sounds True is your trusted partner. At SoundsTrue.com you will find a wealth of free resources to support your journey, including exclusive weekly audio interviews, free downloads, interactive learning tools, and other special savings on all our titles.

To learn more, please visit SoundsTrue.com/freegifts or call us toll-free at 800.333.9185.